RHODESIA: Little White Island

THE VITAL STATISTICS

POPULATION

Africans*	5,220,000
Europeans	249,000
Coloureds**	16,900
Asians	9,300

* Two thirds live in rural areas   ** Mixed race

Land Tenure Act (1969)

	million acres
National land	6·0
European areas	45·0
African areas	
Tribal Trust land	39·9
Purchase area	3·7

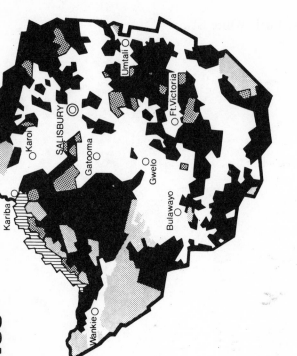

- Much of best agricultural land is European

- All towns are in European areas

Kariba

Wankie

Karoi

SALISBURY

Gatooma

Gwelo

Bulawayo

Ft. Victoria

Umtali

RHODESIA:
Little White Island

John Parker

With a foreword by
Sir Roy Welensky

 Pitman Publishing

First published 1972

Sir Isaac Pitman and Sons Ltd.
Pitman House, Parker Street, Kingsway, London WC2B 5PB
P.O. Box 46038, Portal Street, Nairobi, Kenya

Sir Isaac Pitman (Aust.) Pty. Ltd.
Pitman House, 158 Bouverie Street, Carlton, Victoria 3053, Australia

Pitman Publishing Company S.A. Ltd.
P.O. Box 11231, Johannesburg, South Africa

Pitman Publishing Corporation
6 East 43rd Street, New York, N.Y. 10017, U.S.A.

Sir Isaac Pitman (Canada) Ltd.
495 Wellington Street West, Toronto 135, Canada

The Copp Clark Publishing Company
517 Wellington Street West, Toronto 135, Canada

ISBN: 0 273 36167 8

Printed by photolithography and bound in Great Britain at
The Pitman Press, Bath
(G.3778:11)

Contents

Foreword

BY THE RT HON SIR ROY WELENSKY KCMG

It is an understatement to say that this book of John Parker's is going to be controversial. Here is a man who came to Rhodesia in what one might almost call "the balmy days of peace", before the heady brew of African Nationalism had hit the Central African scene, when the white man's prerogative of power and leadership was almost unquestioned — certainly from the Congo to the Cape.

He saw the rise and fall of the Central African Federation, and he has some unkind things to say about its leaders — including myself. He has, however, proved himself to be a man who is prepared to stand by what, he believes, are the principles which should govern his life.

The story of his difficulties, both personal and public, as a journalist and eventually in a more senior position on one of Rhodesia's most important newspapers is worth telling, principally for the reason that, when he came to Rhodesia, he was barely politically conscious — however, his stay in Rhodesia was long enough to convert him to one who was acutely aware of the extent to which politics had crept into the every-day life of Rhodesians, black and white.

I must make it clear that I do not agree with a great deal of what the author has written. He has viewed events from an angle, and honestly and firmly believes that what he expresses as events, and the reasons for them, are the honest truth; and, knowing him, I accept this; but nonetheless, many of his assumptions are wrong. I give one example — his version of the part which Lord Malvern played in the choice of his successor as Prime Minister of Southern Rhodesia, when Lord Malvern moved to the Federal field.

The facts are that Lord Malvern played no part in the choice of Mr Garfield Todd as his successor. This was done by a Congress at Bulawayo, and an important factor in the ultimate choice of Mr Todd was that the most likely contender, Mr Julian Greenfield, was lukewarm about continuing in Rhodesian politics, and wanted to "go Federal". A group called the Action Group, which worked within the framework of Lord Malvern's United Party, were principally responsible for the choosing of Mr Todd.

I had it several years later from Lord Malvern himself that, if he'd had a preference at that time — and in fact he left me with the impression he hoped it would happen — it was that Sir George Davenport would have been chosen to lead Rhodesia. The facts as I give them could, of course, only be known to those who were among the inner circle.

Now, whilst I have made it clear that there is a great deal in this book which I think is open to challenge, and much of it is going to be resented intensely by Rhodesians, I believe it is a fundamental principle of any democratic state that individuals have the right to hold their own opinions, and any man is entitled to say, "These are the circumstances as I saw them, and I have formed my opinions on these assumptions." For this reason, therefore, I feel that John Parker has every right to express these views and, whether one agrees or disagrees with them, they should be read.

Salisbury:
26 October, 1971

CHAPTER ONE

People Like Us...

To justify yet another book about Rhodesia is probably more difficult than merely writing one. Hundreds of thousands of words have been written about the reasons for, the steps leading to, and the consequences of Ian Smith's Unilateral Declaration of Independence. The Rhodesian way of life has been eulogised, criticised or lambasted (depending on the standpoint of the writer) from every point of the analytical compass. The strengths and weaknesses of the hard-line White supremacists, the middle-of-the-road men, the liberals and the Nationalists have been probed on countless occasions by writers more eminent, more knowledgeable and more intimately connected with events than I.

And yet, I have a tale to tell. It has not been told in full, and I suggest that this itself makes it of interest. But the details of the story are less important than what I hope they will show, which is how a police state could be conceived, born and nursed into full being by a community of ordinary people — "People like us."

There is no bigger fool in the world today than a White Rhodesian. For a quarter of my lifetime to date, I was one of them, so I write not from a sense of superiority but from one of involvement. I was there, I .saw it all happening, and yet I and thousands like me did little or nothing, certainly by no means enough, to stop it. We saw, but did not believe. We could not understand that, in the name of preserving their precious Rhodesian Way of Life, White Rhodesians themselves would systematically set about destroying the very basis upon which it was founded.

My involvement in Rhodesia began on an August day in 1954 when I dropped in to the London office of the Argus Company of South Africa at 85 Fleet Street, to apply for a job as a sub-editor in Bloemfontein. The Argus Company publishes newspapers all over Southern Africa and although the Bloemfontein post was filled, in its place they offered me a post in Rhodesia. I took it.

At the time I was working as a sub-editor on the Press Association, on another floor of the same building as the Argus Company's London Office. It was a night job, and the business of coping with long hours, poor pay and bringing up three young children in a flat in Finchley was beginning to get both Margaret and me down. The Argus Company offered me just over £1,000 a year in Bulawayo, Southern Rhodesia, and it sounded like heaven. This was the time when the "Land of Opportunity" poster really meant something when it was displayed in the window of Rhodesia House in the Strand. Hand in hand, we went along to look — and to read up in the pamphlets and reference books on what was in store for us.

At that time the Federation of Rhodesia and Nyasaland had been formed a year or so before. Sir Godfrey Huggins, the architect of the Federation, was Federal Prime Minister. We read of his new policy of "partnership", which to our inexperienced ears sounded the magical formula for success in race relations. In "partnership" with our African brothers, we would help build the future in the Central African sun. Assisted of course, as was carefully pointed out by Tony Anthony, a smooth young man who later became a senior Federal Civil Servant, by the servants whom every white family quite naturally employed.

We read about the Federation, the "partnership" of the

two Rhodesias and Nyasaland. We were told of the unlimited economic prospects of this great new association, greater than half Europe in size and promising to match if not surpass the riches of South Africa herself. Not for Rhodesia, we were told, the policies of apartheid which were already beginning to gnaw at the roots of South Africa's membership of the British Commonwealth of Nations. Rhodesia was led by Garfield Todd, Huggins's nominee, the brightest and most intelligent liberal politician south of the Sahara. Yes, said Mr Anthony, I'm sure you'll do very well there. You'll be bound to have a car — "all Europeans have cars" — and cigarettes are only 2s 9d for fifty. Fifty! And the Africans? Not a sign of trouble for sixty years. The most peaceful, likeable lot in the world. You'll have no trouble with your servants.

The point I am trying to make is that Margaret and I, and our children, were nothing special. We were simply among the thousands of settlers (pejorative word though this has become) who went to Africa from Britain to try to make a new life for ourselves in the sun. We had no sense of reforming zeal; no particular liberal or socialist inclinations. In fact, the only conscious political acts I had committed up to the age of 27 had been to vote Conservative and to assist, during one election campaign, to paint the local Labour Party's office blue. Innocents abroad indeed, in many more senses than one. We left behind a drab, grey Britain struggling to overcome the effects of two world wars and disillusioned by the non-arrival of the "new Elizabethan era" the newspapers and the politicians had promised us. We knew very little of the country which was to become our home for the next eleven years; not much more than a smattering of history overlaid with Kiplingesque romanticism about the "immense and brooding spirit" of Cecil John Rhodes, father and founder of Rhodesia. "Living, he was the land . . ." And all that. We had no knowledge of the real history of the African peoples of Southern Africa, and practically no experience of mixing — or not mixing — with a foreign race of a different colour. Three-and-a-half years in the British Army at the end of the war had taken me through France to the Middle East, and to some idea that the Wogs did not actually start at Calais. Service in Palestine had also destroyed some well-nurtured myths of the infallibility of British authority held since schooldays; while Margaret's experience as a nurse had also minimally broadened her outlook on racial matters. We both recall with respect and affection a brilliant Indian woman doctor in Nuneaton whose intelligence and erudition far outshone our own. The fact that she was also a Communist (the first we had actually talked to) shocked us only slightly. We would have reacted with surprise and some horror to any suggestion that we were in any way racially biased, and I hope and believe that this was and still is true. But in the mid-1950s, the simple truth was that we had never found ourselves in any situation where race had affected us in any way. We didn't know there was anything to be biased about. To average members of the nation that had stood up so gallantly to the horrors of Nazism, anything which suggested prejudice of a racial, religious or any other brand was unthinkable.

So we didn't think of it. We sold up whatever of our small possessions were saleable, gave away the remainder, signed all the forms, procured a passport, and prepared to set sail for Cape Town. We had one-way tickets, a trunk-load of clothes, a carry-cot for the baby and £63 10s to transfer to the bank in Bulawayo. It wasn't much on which to start a new life.

Before we left, there was one insignificant incident. By a coincidence, our successors at the flat in Finchley had just returned to Britain from Northern Rhodesia, now Zambia. I spent half an hour or so going over the inventory with the wife of the new tenant, whose name I cannot recall but who was vastly intrigued to learn that we were emigrating.

"You'll never stand it," she said, positively. "The natives are terrible. They steal all the time."

I expressed interest.

"Oh yes," she said. "You will find your sugar bill goes up by double every week. The servants steal it all. If you don't want to lose everything your wife will have to go round with a bunch of keys on her belt like a jailer. I couldn't stand it. That's why we've come back."

We were to learn that this woman's attitude was by no means an uncommon one among white Rhodesian housewives; but at the time, we paid little enough attention. We were off on our great adventure.

It is impossible to exaggerate the initial effect that Rhodesia had on us, and some explanation of our circumstances is necessary at this point to explain the violent contrast between our new life and what we had experienced in England. We had been married some seven years, and had three sons under the age of five. We had travelled around the country seeking a satisfactory job and reasonable accommodation within our means, but the blunt truth was that although my work was reasonably well regarded wherever I went, few young journalists make a fortune. The winter of 1954/55 was one of the coldest on record this century in London, and we could not afford to heat adequately the vast and gloomy flat that was the only accommodation we could find. To make ends meet, I was forced to work long hours of overtime; and I would return grey-faced and exhausted at four and five o'clock in the morning after leaving for the office some 18 hours before. To add to our joys, the flat acquired a poltergeist which, night after night, switched on a very stiff electric light switch in an untenanted attic and scared Margaret half out of her wits . . .

We left England on a cold and misty day in February 1955, with frost on the ground and rime along the handrails of the old *Stirling Castle,* veteran of the Southampton run to Cape Town. Just under three weeks later, the boat train from Cape Town disgorged us on to the longest platform in the world at Bulawayo station on a velvet dark night; the next morning we were taken by car to the house my company had found for us for the first few weeks of our time in Rhodesia.

The timing couldn't have been better. It was March, coming up towards the end of the rainy season, when everything is green and the long days of unbroken sunshine give way to star-studded nights murmurous with crickets. After London in February, the colours bedazzled. Bougainvillea in orange, yellow, purple; violent scarlet tulip trees; multi-coloured cannas waving their flags; green grass everywhere, sprouting its runners across the surface of the rust-red ground to take root and shoot out again. The temperature; high seventies by day, mid-sixties by night. Not too hot for comfort, or for sleep at night.

The house we were shown belonged to the firm's advertising manager, who was away on holiday for a few weeks. Subsidised, we could stay there until we found our feet and our own accommodation. Compared with our Finchley flat — and anywhere else we'd managed to find in England — it was approaching heaven.

North End is a comfortable European suburb of Bulawayo where there are no millionaires, but no "poor whites" either. The roads are tarred and lined with well-established jacaranda and flame trees. The houses stand neatly by themselves in a third of an acre, more or less, and with very few exceptions they are all of bungalow construction. Only in the very centres of the cities is *lebensraum* scarce enough in Rhodesia for blocks of flats. The endless terraces of the outskirts of any town in Britain are nowhere to be seen in Rhodesia. There are other, different and worse types of housing, to be sure, but on this our first day in the country we were not aware of them. Nor did we want to be. They are not for those of Caucasian origin.

Our house stood in a shady street named after the founder of the Boy Scout movement. Knowing Rhodesians as I do now, I am inclined to believe more that it was named for Lord Baden Powell's exploits as a soldier in the South African War than for the benevolent paternalism which crosses so many racial barriers. But Baden Powell Road was peaceful enough, and our bungalow looked to us like paradise. There was a semi-circular drive up to the front door, lined with frangipane trees, whose white-pink-and-yellow blossoms put Chanel to shame. Here and there an orange tree, with ripe fruit hanging ready to pluck, stood out among the flowering shrubs. Inside the glass front door, we could see the shining parquet flooring stretching through the house into the living-cum-dining room, with its sliding partition. Scatter rugs on the floor, unfussy Colonial furniture with wide wooden arms (admirable stands for beer glasses and bottles) held out a comfortable welcome. We tiptoed in disbelief through the wide kitchen, with its humming refrigerator (we'd never been able to afford one in England) the white bathroom and the cool bedrooms with their ornately whirligigged burglar-bars. Everything was white and light, and we were happy.

As if to confirm our conviction that for once in our lifetime all was right with the world, there came a knock at the front door. There stood an African lady of considerable proportions, a beaming white smile on her large black face, and a tray carrying tea, milk, cups and saucers and home-made cake. She also bore a message from her mistress, our next-door neighbour out of sight behind the frangipane. Would we excuse her for sending this round? She knew how tired we must be after our journey and did not wish to impose herself on us. But anything she could do ...

It was not the last kindness that we received from Kathleen Robb and her husband Ken. Their welcome to a strange family from far away, who had so obviously not washed the green from behind their ears, could not have been warmer. I am glad that we moved from their neighbourhood long before I began to get involved in political attitudes (strike them, some people may well say) for this would have inevitably led to arguments and ill-feeling. Their instant friendliness and that of other people in the street (my editor, who lived a few doors down, sent round half a bottle of sherry that night with a similar sort of message) did much to help us settle down with record speed.

Rhodesia, we felt, was where we belonged. We might have no money, but we had a job, we had a roof over our heads for the time being at least, and while the sun shone it just wasn't worth being miserable. Not for the last time, we came to the conclusion that if one is to be poor, one might as well be so in a warm climate. We began to launch out. We took bus rides into the city centre, finding to our surprise that the buses were segregated, cramped wooden seats for Africans separated by a partition from not-so-spartan upholstery for Europeans. I can still recall a slight sense of shock at realising that in 1955 Cape Town was far more liberal in outlook than Bulawayo, at least as far as municipal transport was concerned.

Only two days after our arrival, we acquired our first African servant — houseboy, as we quickly learned to call him. He was a smoothly good-looking man of about 30 who, to our relief, spoke excellent English and knew his job well. We were slightly in awe of him — he was very superior and our previous experience of servants extended as far as employing the infrequent char — and he had two habits which we found strange. The first was to spend hours every evening catching and eating — live — the great, green, locust-like grasshoppers which swarmed around the street-light outside our garden. The second was pilfering, which was simple enough from an inexperienced couple such as us, but we learned fast enough to part company with David, for that was what he called himself, after a month.

Whether David had a wife or family, I never knew. I didn't ask. He lived in the "kia", as the servants quarters are known throughout Southern Africa. It simply means "room". David's was better than most, as we were to learn through the years. It consisted of an unplastered brick room built on to the garage, seven feet by seven feet by seven feet, furnished by a bed with the bare minimum of steel springing and a mattress. He brought his own blankets, cooked his own food on a primus stove provided by us (he was permitted to cook our food in our kitchen on our electric stove, but not his own) and had what were euphemistically known as "separate toilet facilities." This meant a cold water "shower" in a 2ft. by 2ft. box which also had a hole in the floor. Many Africans, we were told by those we felt should know, were not civilised enough to use a lavatory with a seat. They preferred to squat . . .

One such authority was the genial giant who was another neighbour. Like David, he also frightened us timid newcomers, although in a different way. David had been with us a couple of hours, and we were revelling in the "luxury" of being waited on for the first time, when a cheerful hail took me across to his fence.

Our new friend was well over six feet tall and burly with it. He wore khaki shorts to just above mid-thigh, and a short-sleeved shirt with pockets on the breast. Muscular tanned thighs and biceps bulged (he had played rugby for the Transvaal, I believe) and he addressed me in the guttural Afrikaans accent which it is impossible to reproduce in print.

He introduced himself.

"Just out from the old country, eh?"

"Yes."

"Been in Africa before?"

"Not really, Egypt, for a bit . . ."

"Ah." Pause. "So you don't know about Africans, then?"

"What do you mean?"

"See you've got a boy then."

"Yes, we've got three sons, actually."

"No, *house* boy. But don't you worry. You have any trouble with him, just bring him to me. I'm in the African Education Department and I can hit them so the police don't see. Come and have a snifter."

It would not be true to pretend that the conversation made a stronger impression on me than to leave a vague unease. But it has stayed fresh in my memory, like it or not, over the years so I suppose it must have meant something, even at the time. But for the Parker family, as for the thousands of other immigrants, the last thing to worry about was the African in Rhodesia. He was there, convenient, irritating, smiling, insolent, hardworking or shiftless, however one found him. But he wasn't our concern. We had no reforming zeal to improve his lot, no wish or need to meet Jim Fish or Mrs Fish. In fact, it was more than seven years before we entertained an African family in our own home for the first (and last) time. It is not a record we are proud of, nor for that matter particularly ashamed of. Beyond a mild resolve to treat our servants well and, within reason, generously — which like many good resolutions we often failed to fulfil — we had no feelings at all. There was far too much for us to do in establishing ourselves in our new country, fighting off the ever-pressing bills, setting up home, finding new schools, begging and borrowing furniture, mastering a new job and making new friends. But in those first tentative years in Bulawayo, Lobengula's former capital, we made the groping beginnings to try to meet and know and to understand the extraordinary society which had accepted us so readily into its circle.

Very broadly speaking, this fell into three categories, each capable of being broken down into any number of sub-sections. There were Pre-War Rhodesians (White); Post-War or New Rhodesians (White) and Kaffirs (Black). There was also the twilight fringe of what is called in Rhodesia the Coloured Community (the unhappy products of miscegenation) and those members of the Moslem fraternity and their descendants from Pakistan and India who were always referred to as "Eyeshuns."

In the category of Pre-War Rhodesians must be included of course their offspring. By and large they made up the Establishment from which were drawn the governments of the Federation and its three territories. It was carefully explained to me on my first day with the *Bulawayo Chronicle.* At the top of the Rhodesian social ladder came the Pioneers (Capital P). These were the gentlemen (and occasional lady) who had been members of the 1890 Column which first colonised the territory or possibly had arrived earlier. Early Settlers (Capital E S) arrived between 1893 and 1896. And third down the ladder were early settlers (lower case e s) who had been so fortunate as to arrive before the turn of the century. In the nature of things some 55 to 65 years later there were only a few of these venerable figures left, even at the start of our stay in Rhodesia.

Of course it is unfair to generalise, but in the main Pre-War Rhodesians tended to be rich, farmers or traders, have undistinguished offspring whom they sent (if male) to Plumtree or St. George's, the Rhodesian Eton and Harrow. Occasionally they turned out to be poor, feckless and living and dying in squalor in one of the corrugated iron-roofed shanties in the older roads, their minds sapped by the sun, their money sunk in cheap Cape brandy, and their habitations eaten away by white ants.

The Post-War Rhodesians, of whom we were the latest examples, were beginning to make their weight felt in society. This was the time when immigration reached its peak of 20,000 a year for a short period, and although the bulk of us came either from Britain or South Africa, there was a substantial infusion of Greeks, Italians, Germans and Scandinavians. We were a polyglot crowd. The man with whom I used to tire both the sun and the moon with talking was a White Russian Jew, educated at an American university in Shanghai, who had fought for the Israeli Army and had come to Rhodesia to find peace.

It was an exciting time. Rhodesia, tucked away behind its barriers of time and distance for so long, was brimming over with activity. The mood was expansion. Capital and people were flooding in, bringing with them new outlooks and novel ideas. For ten years Salisbury, once described to me by a Rhodesian as "the town where the prevailing disease is an ingrowing mind" became the cosmopolitan capital of Africa south of the Sahara. It is strange now to recall how real it all was, when so much of it has turned out to be illusion. The Federation, that was to bring the economic millenium to Central Africa; Partnership, under which the races would march together forward into the future, an example to the world. Both sunk almost without trace. The British tradition, so widely trumpeted, of justice and fair play, submerged almost without a struggle and re-emerging as the Nazi tradition of the Master-Race.

It happened in the eleven years my family and I spent in Rhodesia, a short enough span in terms of a lifetime and shorter still in terms of a country's history. How it took place, and why, have been told and retold a thousand times in the Press, on television and in scores of volumes. The purpose of this book is to try to explain how the lives and characters of perfectly ordinary folk like ourselves were affected by those events.

CHAPTER TWO

More British
than the British

All communities are to some extent bound by their past;
after all, the present is founded on it. White Rhodesians,
Old and New, are swathed to the eyebrows with their
history, perhaps because there is not much of it. In 1967,
two years after UDI, a television executive in Rhodesia
who had left in disgust to live in London received a letter
from his former boss in Salisbury. It offered him a job
better than his old one, at vastly enhanced salary, and
went on:

"What we are trying to do here now is to re-create the
Rhodesia of the 1920s and '30s. I am sure we will succeed,
and I am sure you are the man to help us do so."

Apart from the attitude of facing what is to come with
your eyes firmly fixed on what may have happened forty
years ago, the remarkable thing about this letter is that it
was written by a man who himself became a Rhodesian
only in 1960! There is no reason to doubt his sincerity. I
am sure he meant every word he wrote from the bottom of
his heart. But the fact remains that in 1970, three years
after writing the letter, its author himself was back in
London, looking for a job. Perhaps he found the task of
re-creating the past beyond him.

The point about Rhodesia and its past is that, since the
day that Cecil Rhodes's emissaries persuaded King

Lobengula to sign the Rudd Concession, permitting the white man to mine for gold and other minerals, Rhodesia has been living a lie. The white man originally took control of the country by a trick, and ever since then has indulged in any number of historical self-deceptions designed to perpetuate the supremacy of white over black, the myth by which Rhodesia has lived since 1890.

Any white Rhodesian will tell you that the African has contributed nothing to the advancement of himself, or the world, through the centuries. Before the white man came to Rhodesia, you can be sure, Matabele were slaughtering Mashona by the thousand, and the white man's only purpose was to pacify the country so that he could mine it. To hear the Rhodesian tell it, the Mashona people were on the verge of being eliminated by the "murdering Matabele hordes" when the just and generous white man took over and brought peace to a troubled land. Since then, the white man's skills and the white man's taxes have added prosperity to peace, and now, eighty years later, there are five million Africans where once they scarce numbered half a million.

Before the white man came to Rhodesia the country was mainly populated by two tribes. The larger and longer-established were the Mashona, who occupied the land for centuries and whose ancestors probably built the medieval fortress near Fort Victoria now known as Zimbabwe. It is now generally accepted that these fascinating ruins form concrete evidence that hundreds of years ago the Africans of the centre of the continent organised and ran their own complex civilisation. The golden empire of Monomotapa may well have been the source of the untold riches of the Queen of Sheba.

Whatever the glories of their past, the Mashona in the late nineteenth century had fallen upon hard times. They were totally dominated by their less numerous but much tougher neighbours, the Matabele. These warriors, off-shoots of the Zulu nation, swept north in the first half of the century. Their chief, Mzilikaze, had incurred the disfavour of Chaka, the great king who had knit the disjointed Bantu tribes of South Africa into a national unit. After brushing with the Boers, at the time themselves occupied with their "treks" north from the Cape, Mzilikaze settled with his warriors in what is now known as Matabeleland, and, true to his custom, proceeded to subjugate his neighbours the Mashona, a mild and inoffensive people. Their villages were subject to periodic raiding by Matabele impis, their women and their cattle were carried off and their young men killed.

Horrific as this practice sounds, there is no evidence whatsoever that the Mashona were being subjected to systematic genocide, as the modern white Rhodesian would have you believe. There is more evidence to suggest that the Mashona were prepared to submit to the occasional raids by the forces of a dominant chief like Mzilikazi or Lobengula than they were the subtle and insidious presence of the white man, who came upon their land by stealth and then, before they realised what had happened, assumed control and suppressed opposition by force.

The Occupation of Rhodesia has been fully documented elsewhere many times, but it is necessary at least to sketch in the outlines of what Rhodesians regard as their propitious beginnings.

Nineteenth-century Africa was dominated by the discovery of diamonds at Kimberley and gold on the Rand in Transvaal. These in turn were themselves dominated by Cecil John Rhodes, the son of an English country parson and the least likely of all men, apparently, to achieve greatness. At the age of 17 he went to Africa for the sake of his health. He had weak lungs, and indeed these were to kill him before he reached fifty. But the sickly boy outmanouevred the Victorian moguls and the adventurers who flocked from all over the world to share in the new wealth. He amassed a tremendous fortune himself, became Prime Minister of the Cape Colony, and founded the Chartered Company to further his dream of spreading the British flag north to the Mediterranean. An echo of his hopes can today be found in Lusaka, whose main street is still named "Cairo Road"

The history of Rhodes's machinations to obtain the Rudd Concession from the Matabele King Lobengula makes sad reading. Robert Moffatt, a Scottish missionary, had won the friendship and confidence of Mzilikaze, Lobengula's father, and Rhodes with cool calculation sent Moffatt's son John, following in his father's evangelistic footsteps, to the court of Lobengula to trade on his father's trust. It was not quite like shooting a sitting rabbit, for Lobengula, primitive and uneducated though he was, was a crafty ruler who foresaw pretty clearly the menace of the white man's advance. Moffatt persuaded Lobengula to repudiate a tentative agreement he had signed previously with the Boers of the Transvaal, and to put his thumb-print instead on a mutual protection treaty with the British. The subsequent protection that the invading British columns received from Lobengula was considerable. In return, Lobengula was first tricked into allowing the white columns within his territory, next his brave young men were slaughtered by the Maxim gun, and finally his capital was surrounded and he himself forced to flee into the bush to die. Rhodes's "protection" would seem to have served as an excellent model for the latter-day excesses of the Mafiosa.

After the missionaries, Rhodes sent in the businessmen. With Moffatt and another missionary, C.D. Helm (also paid by Rhodes) advising him and certifying his character, Rhodes's "agent" C.D. Rudd, obtained the famous piece of paper which assigned him "and his heirs and successors" the right to mine for metals and minerals.

Rhodesians have always been conscious that the pen, indeed, can be mightier than the sword. Rhodes promptly persuaded the British Government that Rudd's document was his charter to occupy Lobengula's empire. Britain's policy at the time was Imperialistic and she had no intention of being left behind when it came to sharing the spoils of the great African carve-up. Rhodes got his backing, and the Chartered Company was born.

It was of course the promise of Mashonaland's gold

which attracted investors to the Company. And it was a precisely similar promise which Rhodes held out to the 700 motley individuals he recruited to form the Pioneer Column which finally settled on the site of what is now Salisbury in 1890. It is perhaps significant that Rhodesia's road has been littered with broken promises of one sort or another since the very beginning. Lobengula thought he was signing way the right of a few men to dig holes in the ground; the Pioneers believed they were destined to make fortunes in return for a slightly risky few months' ride. The Chartered Company's investors were led to believe their millions would reap billions and burnish the lustre of the British Crown. Lobengula lost his warriors, his cattle, his kingdom and his life. The Pioneers made hardly a golden sovereign to rub between them; it was not until modern machinery and methods could be imported years later that anyone earned more than a few shillings out of Rhodesia's gold, and then most of it was found under the ancient workings of the despised Africans. Rhodes's Company failed to pay a dividend for over thirty years, which must have pleased the investors no end; and far from bringing honour to the British Crown the Rhodesian adventure culminated seventy-odd years later in messy and idiotic rebellion.

Occupation Day is a solemn occasion in white Rhodesia — a day of martial music, flagpole ceremonies and special prayers under the jacaranda trees of Salisbury's Cecil Square. For the Pioneers who drove the first Column through Lobengula's kingdom to make laager under the lee of Harare Kopje (hill) are the recipients of a kind of reverence they neither deserved or would have expected. The late Frank Clements, a latter-day Mayor of Salisbury whose excellent book "Rhodesia: The Course to Collision" contains probably the most succinct, penetrating and understandable account of those early days, quotes a tough old storekeeper's reply to Rhodes's appeal to his idealism: "I'll have you know, Mr Rhodes, I did not come here for posterity."

The Column consisted of 200 volunteers recruited in

South Africa from more than 2,000 applicants tempted by the offer of 1,500 morgen (more than 3,000 acres) of land and 15 free mining claims apiece. With them went an "escort" of 500 "police", who would today be described as mercenaries. Organised under regular military officers and on military lines, the Escort contained as extraordinary a mixture of adventurers as ever got together under a pirate's flag.

Indeed, the whole expedition had something of the piratical about it — the smack of danger, the venture into the unknown, the promise of untold riches at the end of the trail. Looking back now, perhaps the most surprising of all their achievements was that they stayed long enough to establish the community that Rhodes was banking on as his outpost of Empire.

That they arrived at all was largely due to the forbearance of Lobengula, who stubbornly resisted the wishes of his impis to attack the white man. So as not to provoke an open confrontation with the warriors who had faced and beaten British troops only a few years before in open battle, the Column skirted Lobengula's strongholds in Matabeleland and, led by the white hunter Selous, headed for the high veld of Mashonaland. There was no resistance from the Mashonas, already cowed into subservience by the Matabele raiders, and indeed it seems likely that some of the Mashona tribe at first welcomed the white man's guns as protection against the long spears of the Matabele.

Once he was in, however, the white man proved impossible to dislodge. Settlements were quickly established as the miners spread themselves around, looking for gold, and the farmers began carving a livelihood out of the fertile bush. Quickly the Mashonas found themselves the unknowing victims of the white man's cash economy. Oversimplified, it went like this. The white man wanted (and needed) the African's labour in order to dig his mine or work his land. But the African, accustomed to centuries of subsistence farming, had no desire (or need) to work for a living. Without putting too fine a point on it, if the white man was not to press the black into direct slavery, which would have been hardly possible or politic even in the 1890s, then he had to create in the black both the desire and the need for money. The white man's luxuries, his guns, his liquor, his way of life, could only be purchased for hard cash. The Mashona had nothing to sell except their labour.

But there was something else, too. The Charter granted by the British Government authorised the Company to set up an administration to run the new territories. The Administration needed cash on which to run itself, so it promptly imposed taxes on all those living in the area over which it claimed authority. Not very much indeed — just a few shillings a head each year — but so the African was forced into the white man's employ in order to pay the white man's tax. So the cycle was complete, and in all basic principles has remained so ever since.

One of the proudest boasts of White Rhodesia is that, until the "nationalist-inspired riots" in Salisbury and Bulawayo in 1960, not a single life had been taken by the internal security forces. The lessons meted out in response to the Matebele and Mashona "rebellions" in 1893 and 1896 were strong ones indeed.

It suits modern Rhodesians to refer to both events as "rebellions". In fact, the 1893 affair was the inevitable ultimate clash between Lobengula and the white intruders that he had postponed by his forbearance three years before. In spite of the establishment of the white communities of Salisbury, Fort Victoria and other places, Lobengula still claimed for his impis the right to raid the Mashona. This they did, by and large leaving the whites alone. Mashonaland's first Administrator, Dr Jameson, believed firmly and probably correctly that the white man would never be secure in Rhodesia until Lobengula's power was broken and the Company's rule extended to cover Matebeleland as well. He had no compunction at using the periodic Matabele raids (which admittedly he could do little to stop) to force a showdown with Lobengula and using his light artillery and the Maxim gun

to mow down the impis at long range. Many of the
Matabele had never faced gunfire before and some of them
showed fanatical bravery in the face of devastating
firepower. Lobengula burned down his headquarters and
fled, having first with remarkable tolerance ensured the
safety of the white traders who had been trapped with
him.

Lobengula was reputed to have taken with him in his
flight the bulk of his treasure and it appears to have been
this fact, rather than any pressing military necessity, that
tempted Major Allan Wilson and his Patrol of 33 men to
venture after them into the thick bush near the Shangani
River. They died to a man, and it was their fate which has
inspired the most lasting and remarkable Rhodesian legend
of all. Their remains lie under the wide skies at World's
View, in the Matopos Hills, not thirty yards from the
bones of Cecil Rhodes himself. It is not too far from the
truth to suggest that in white Rhodesia's hierarchy of
religious idols, God comes 35th, although not one
Rhodesian in a thousand could repeat the name of a single
member of the Patrol.

The Matebele were defeated with very heavy losses.
Some reports put the number at 5,000 tribesmen slain, but
one estimate is as good or as bad as the next. What is
certain is that, apart from Major Wilson's ill-fated Patrol,
white losses were extremely small. This was far from the
case in the totally unexpected Mashona uprising which
followed some three years later. This was largely inspired
by the Mlimi priests, whose influence had grown sharply
since the defeat of the Matabele. It was the first example
of Rhodesia's Africans combining in a genuine national
movement to try to be rid of the white man's yoke, and
the lessons learned then have weighed heavily on
Rhodesia's history ever since.

In the first place, the uprising was far less gentlemanly
from the white man's point of view. This time there was
no casual massacre of the valiant savage at long range from
behind the comfortable sights of a Maxim gun. Death came
in the night, by the knife and the panga, to women and

children as well as men, and more than one-tenth of the
4,000 Europeans then in the Colony died in the first
month or two of the fighting. The rebellion caught the
whites at precisely the wrong time. Dr Jameson had
denuded Rhodesia of both men and horses to take part in
the ill-fated Jameson Raid on the Rand. (This was the
miscalculation that led to his ignominious surrender at
Doornkop with all his men, to the ending of Cecil
Rhodes's Premiership of the Cape and to the decline of the
great man's influence in British politics.)

Militarily, the result in retrospect was never in doubt.
The white men grouped themselves for the last time into
their famous Boer-type *laagers* in Salisbury and Bulawayo
and other white centres, and waited for help from the
South in the form of Imperial troops. This was readily
forthcoming, but it took more than 18 months before
Rhodesia was pacified. Cecil Rhodes demonstrated not
only his courage but also his great political skill in meeting
with the Matabele at a great indaba in the Matopos and
bringing much of the fighting to an end by his personal
intervention. He certainly averted what would probably
have been a long and bitter guerrilla struggle.

This was the last time for many years that Rhodesia
made World (or even British) headlines. After the first
turbulent decade, the country settled down at the dawn of
the new century to some fifty years of steady, if
unspectacular development. Rhodes died in 1902, and the
descriptions of his death and the last rites in the Matopos
Hills filled many columns of the *Bulawayo Chronicle*. His
body was brought from Cape Town on the new railway,
which only five years before had been pushed across the
scrub of Bechuanaland to Bulawayo, and which had
extended north to the copper mines of what is now
Zambia and east to Salisbury. The troubles of the
Anglo-South African War passed Rhodesia by, just as the
convulsions of the First World War left her virtually
unscathed. By now the ingredients of the Rhodesian
tragedy had been sown and were well and truly rooted.
The white assumption of supremacy had immigrated with

the Columns from South Africa. Many of the early settlers were Boers, who brought their fiery puritanism and blinkered paternalism along with their hausfraus. To the white man, the defeat of the tribes had given added proof, if such were needed, of his supremacy. But the atrocities committed by both sides in the fighting were never forgotten, even 70 years later.

An attitude of resentment towards authority in general, and to British authority in particular, thrived among the independently-minded settlers. The majority were of British origin who, by being in Rhodesia at all, mentally had already thrown off their traditional shackles. Certainly from the very start Britain exercised, if only minimally, a cautionary rein on Rhodesia's freedom of action, particularly in so far as the Africans were concerned. Early newspaper reports (the *Mashonaland Times,* Rhodesia's first newspaper, started in 1891 only a few months after the first occupation) are full of accounts of settler dissatisfaction with both the Company administration and with Colonial Office influence.

After the Jameson Raid, Britain stationed Imperial officers in the company territory. A Resident-General was sent to safeguard African interests, and a Commandant-General to control the armed police and military and to prevent any further politico-military adventures like the famous Raid. The early settlers spent a large part of their time warring with both these and the Company officials, and endeavouring to take over control of their own affairs.

By 1922 they were at least 90 per cent successful. In the 30-odd years since the Occupation the white population had grown from 1,500 in 1891 to 35,000. It was no longer possible for the Company to control either politically or administratively the large and growing colony, and in 1915, the year when the Charter was first reviewed, a clause had been written in allowing for "responsible government" if and when the white inhabitants should ever ask for it. After a bitter referendum campaign, they voted substantially for it, by 8,774 to 5,989, rejecting the alternative of absorption by South Africa, which both

General Smuts and the British Colonial Secretary, Winston Churchill, advocated.

It is interesting to note that the franchise upon which the vote was based bears no mention of race. The qualifications had been imposed in 1898 and were those then in force in the Cape Colony, from which so much of Rhodesian law was adopted. The vote could be claimed by all male British subjects or all males who had made a declaration of allegiance, provided that:

1. They were over 21
2. They were able to fill in the application form by themselves in English
3. They owned a mining claim of occupied property worth £75 or had an income of £50 a year.

By 1919 the franchise had been extended to women over 21 who could qualify on the basis of their husband's property; the property qualification had been raised to £150 and the income qualification to £100.

Sixty Africans were on the voters' roll.

Frank Clements draws a close and interesting comparison between the voters of 1922 and those of 1965 who lined up for and against Ian Smith's UDI. In 1922 the choice was between union with South Africa and "Responsible Government". In 1965 it was between continued subordination to Britain and so-called "Independence". In 1922 the line-up for union was formidable indeed. It included most of the Civil Service, whose whole system had been based upon and staffed by immigrants from, the Cape system. They were South African-orientated, as was the Press, which was almost totally South African-owned, and did a strong job in both Bulawayo and Salisbury in pressing the claims of union. The private commercial and mercantile interests were strongly biased towards South Africa, where they were mostly founded and with whom they had preferential tariff links, and the bigger mining interests, all heavily South African-controlled, also favoured union. In fact the whole of the "Establishment", points out Clements, was opposed to "Responsible Government" and was defeated by a combination of farmers, small businessmen and artisans. The "go it alone" spirit was alive in white Rhodesia in 1922 as it was in 1965, and sheer bloody mindedness played just as large a part on both occasions.

"Responsible Government" in 1922 meant what it said. The new Rhodesian legislature of 30 members took over complete internal government of the Colony, including responsibility for the police and the armed forces. But Britain reserved to herself considerable powers in all matters concerning the Africans, external affairs (which might affect her treaty obligations), and possibly the most powerful "reservation" of all, the appeal from the Rhodesian High Court to the Privy Council. Over the years, these powers were never exercised overtly; Lord Malvern (Huggins) used to say that most political matters were talked over in discreet privacy before ever anything like a public policy affecting the voters was announced; and as the years went by the "reserved powers" became ever more symbolic. By the time Ian Smith deemed it necessary to sever all remaining ties with Britain by the crude slash of UDI, their effect was so negligible as to be non-existent as far as the ordinary Rhodesian (white or black) was concerned. If ever the substance was given up for the shadows it was in Rhodesia. Smith and his colleagues created the cry of "independence" in order to gain power. They had had no other policy that would have worked with the electorate at the time. In gaining their "independence", they ended a purely nominal dependence on Britain which, so far as it was ever exercised, served merely to cushion white Rhodesians from the pressure of international public opinion. They chose instead the reality of physical and economic dependence on South Africa and Portugal. They have yet to pay the price for the bargain.

As much as anything else, the 1922 vote for responsible government was a "hands off, South Africa" gesture, largely based on dislike of the Afrikaners who from the start had made up a substantial minority of the European settlement of Rhodesia. Although the two "white tribes" drew together in face of the African tribal threats of the 1890s the Boer-Britain complex was as firmly rooted as the white man himself.

For some reason — possibly sheer scenic sentiment, for parts of Rhodesia do resemble closely some of the more beautiful aspects of Britain — Rhodesia remained in many ways the most British of all the Colonies. She remained firmly loyal to the Crown during the Boer War, sending both men and horses to the fight; and her soldiers performed prodigies of valour in Flanders and Gallipoli during the First World War.

The country became a Mecca for upper class (safe) adventure and middle class settlement, and immigrants from Britain were always welcomed before those from any other nation. Conditions in the Rhodesian Civil Service closely paralleled those in the Colonial Service in other parts of Africa and India, but had the added advantage of being independent of London; as the century wore on and pressures on European settlement grew, Rhodesia became the haven for bronzed refugees from India, Pakistan, Burma, Kenya and the West African countries. In Rhodesia they were able to extend, for a time at least, the conditions of the British Raj under which they had been brought up and which they could not bear to surrender.

Some of the most outspoken exponents of separatism in Rhodesia today are former Anglo-Indians. One of them, William Harper, a one-time leader of the Dominion Party, was a founder-member of the Rhodesian Front and the architect of many of its more outrageously separatist policies.

As the "natives" took over the reins of power throughout the Third World, so discontented settlers who could not come to terms with the new masters drifted down the continént, finding in Rhodesia the kind of life to which they had become accustomed. Rhodesia, they determined, would be the last stop; after Rhodesia there was nowhere else to run apart from South Africa . . .

During the 40-year idyll which succeeded the "responsible

government" vote of 1922, Rhodesia became an escapists' paradise where, for minimal effort, the world outside could be forgotten. The pace of progress, for European and African alike, seldom rose above the canter of the horse and never above that of the model-T Ford. The advent of the motor-car hardly ruffled the surface of the bush; until the 1950s Rhodesians could scarcely be bothered to build a proper road. When the bone-shattering corrugations and the blinding dust of the tracks across the bundu threatened to choke all communications between their cities, they grudgingly built "strips" and offered them to the gods of progress as a sop.

Even when we arrived in Bulawayo in 1955, the full-width (then only 22ft) tarmac road to Salisbury petered out 12 miles from the town. With short intervals for the towns en route, Gwelo, Selukwe and Hartley, the remaining 300-odd miles were "strip" — twin strips of tarmac so spaced that you drove with your wheels on them. When you met an oncoming vehicle, each moved over to place his off-side wheels on the near-side strip. As the verge was invariably loose sand or gravel, this manoeuvre took place in a welter of dust and flying stones, and for many years it was impossible to insure a car windscreen in Rhodesia.

With the constant passing and repassing, and aided by the very heavy rains in season, the shoulders of the roads were continually in need of repair. Often the strips would stand up from the surrounding gravel by a foot or eighteen inches, and to travel on them was a suicidal adventure which added greatly to the Rhodesian charisma; you had to be tough to drive on those roads. When Federation brought wide, 40-foot highways which cut down the time and removed most of the danger from road travel, Rhodesians lamented the passing of their strips with sincere regret; and they still indulge in fearsome head-on collisions at high speed which keep the accident rate one of the highest in the world.

In the same category of "progress" were Bulawayo's storm drains. When the Pioneers humped their ox-wagons across the Kalahari sands and the bushveld to Bulawayo, some far-sighted individual — possibly Rhodes himself — decreed that the streets must be "wide enough to turn an ox-wagon." Hence Bulawayo, scratched out of the bush with no regard for space considerations, is built on a simple grid system with superbly wide streets. In the beginning, the administrative offices were built at the top of the Kopje and the rest of the town sloped gently away down to the banks of the Matcheumhlope River. The "Streets" run along the side of the slope, the "Avenues" directly down it at right angles.

Throughout the rainy season, from October or November through March or April, the whole of Rhodesia is subject to very heavy tropical downpours. Those of Bulawayo, although usually less frequent than those of Salisbury, are nevertheless spectacular, often as much as two to three inches of rain falling in under an hour.

The Pioneers, naturally, did not want periodic floods washing through their houses and shops, and so down the side of every "Avenue" dug a huge open storm drain, through which they drove their oxen with much shouting and profanity. It meant, of course, that progress along the length of any one of Bulawayo's "Streets" was a series of switchbacks, with a looping series of dips down which, during a downpour, a tidal race of water swept two or three feet deep.

Progress and the motor car had brought tarmac and pavements to Bulawayo, but, by 1955, no-one had bothered to devise a means of levelling out the streets and removing the water by underground drain. They had simply laid the tar over the old switchback system, letting the rainwater drain off on the surface. Not only did this render the town impassable during anything over a moderate shower; but the constant bucking kept the car-spring repairers at full stretch. One of my earliest memories of Bulawayo is being marooned inside the *Chronicle* office for an hour during a thunderstorm, watching four piccanins (black and bare-arsed, just as Sir Roy Welensky once described them) swimming happily in the warm, swirling, mud-red water at the roadside.

Things are different now, but change has come only reluctantly. One gathers that in reality Bulawayans preferred them that way, and that the sentiment expressed in the letter to my friend at the start of this chapter — "We want to turn the clock back . . ." — is a very strong facet of the white Rhodesian character.

Life in Rhodesia between the wars — for those of European stock — was one of stagnant progress. There was no bustling multi-national port to stimulate development; there was no internal pressure on land or living space to force labour into urban production complexes; improvements in farming techniques introduced themselves at a leisurely pace.

Africans and Europeans lived peacably enough side by side, servants and masters alike keeping their place in the ordained scheme of things, with little incentive or provocation for either to make changes. Slowly, but inexorably, the European consolidated his hold on the land and his dominance over the local populace. The imposition of the poll-tax, which I have already mentioned, thrust upon the African the necessity to earn his living from the white man. The tax itself brought the white administrators, backed by the very real force of the white man's law, to take over control from the traditional tribal authorities, the chiefs. The missionaries came too, intent on civilising, converting and educating the black races; thus creating and stimulating the need and the demand for the white man's standards in many spheres. Finally, there was the white trader (and the Asian merchant, too) to respond to that demand and supply the material goods to satisfy it.

Although the British Government, the Imperial Power, reserved to itself in the 1922 Constitution all the power it might ever need to protect the interests of the primitive tribesmen over whom it had gained control, it was during the '20s and '30s that the white rulers of Rhodesia consolidated and set in the concrete of usage and conformity the whole basis of white supremacy. It was during these years that the Land Apportionment Act, which laid the foundation for segregation, came into being. Its author was Sir Maurice Carter, the British Civil Servant who also split up Kenya on the basis of what is good must go to the white man, thus bringing about eventually the lush White Highlands and the Kikuyu ghettos which led directly to Mau Mau.

As in Kenya, it was not what Sir Maurice laid down that was at fault, or the motives behind it; it was the use to which it was put. It is hard to see how an Act, based on benevolent paternalism and aimed primarily at protecting the African from predatory white interests and profiteering, could be twisted into the cornerstone of a constitution the overriding object of which is white supremacy. But it was.

In the '20s and '30s, that supremacy was taken for granted by the white Rhodesian. If the black Rhodesian had any feelings, they were either ignored or simply not heard. Only a few of the more percipient politicians, like Godfrey Huggins, had the slightest realisation of what lay beneath the surface of both European and African complacency. And Huggins was the last person to wish to expose it. His personal and political popularity rested on preserving the status quo. That the Rhodesian establishment (the Hugginsbureau as it used to be called) maintained itself without disruption for some 40 years is a tribute at least to his skill in concealing from both races in Rhodesia — and from the outside world — what was actually happening to them.

Looking back, it is astonishing what the white Rhodesians got away with in the name of democracy. Act followed repressive Act with amicable certainty. The Land Apportionment Act split the country irretrievably into black and white areas; the Industrial Conciliation Act of 1934 specifically excluded Africans from the status of employees in wage and industrial agreements negotiated under it, and they were barred access to certain forms of employment in European Areas. The Native Registration Act strengthened the pass system and effectively limited

African commercial activity.

By the time the Second World War came it was possible for an African to work in a European area only in a subordinate category; he could not own a house or a business in a European area; he could not use the same public facilities such as swimming baths, post offices or hotels, and in Salisbury at least a Municipal by-law made it a finable offence for an African not to step off the sidewalk to let a European pass by. Only in the franchise, that shop-window of democracy, did race have no effect on a person's ability to make his way. Race wasn't mentioned here; anyone could have a vote. But the qualifications, educational and financial, made up for the omission. In 1930 only 70 Africans had enrolled on the electoral lists out of a total of some 28,000.

What sort of people were they, who managed to establish and maintain such an arrogant monopoly of privilege? In the first place, as we have seen, they were adventurers out for a quick fortune, mercenaries, cronies of Rhodes, miners, farmers and traders. They were followed soon by the civil servants, tidying up the administrative mess and establishing not only the rule of law but also that strange code of ethics and conduct transmitted by the British Colonial Office to the four quarters of the World.

(I once attended a Colonial Office "board" in search of a Press Officer for Nyasaland, as it was then called. The first question I was asked was: what car did I drive? I said "Humber," omitting to say that it was at least ten years old and on its last legs. I got the job — and then did not take up the offer. We were sent a marvellous little booklet, informing me I would need "six evening dress suits" and explaining the "grade system". It was not until I visited Zomba later that I realised what this really meant. At the top of the mountain, in the fresh cool air, stood the Governor's Residence. His civil servants lived in lessening degrees of opulence and comfort right down the grades. The unfortunate bottom graders dwelt in two-bedroomed houses with one lavatory some two-thirds of the way down the hill in the fever belt. The higher one progressed, the more loos one was entitled to.)

At its best, of course, the British Civil Service has been the envy of the world; and it is fair to say that in many respects the Rhodesian Civil Service embodied from the start many of its best qualities of dedication, selflessness and hard work. Long-sightedness and liberalism however, have never been conspicuous attributes of the Civil Service mind, and in its benevolent paternalism the Rhodesian version, particularly the infuriatingly named Native Affairs Department, remained with ostrich head in the sands of complacency until the political corruption of the Rhodesian Front had destroyed its very core. It was certainly the influence of the civil servants, as much as the residual effect of Rhodes's chauvinism, which turned white Rhodesia in the early part of the century into the ultra-British community it became. "More English than the English", we used to say, and it was far more true of the early years. These were the days when to serve the Empire was every young gentleman's dream and duty, and Rhodesia was the ideal place to come. Its climate was more lenient, its inhabitants more friendly and its dangers less forbidding than those of Canada, Australia or New Zealand. This "Englishism" absorbed most other cultures which imported themselves into Rhodesia for some sixty years. Sir Roy Welensky, whose background as the son of an Afrikaner and a Polish Jew makes him about as English as the Oder-Neisse line, still claims with weighty sincerity to be the real upholder of the "British tradition" in Africa.

The white artisans — the next element in the Rhodesian immigrant build-up — were a conglomerate lot, mainly recruited from South Africa by the railways, which for years remained the country's principal employer. The Afrikaner element in Rhodesia's white population was largely confined to the farming fraternity, establishing little spheres of influence dotted about the land and remaining stubbornly unchanged through the years in both appearance and outlook. To any white Rhodesian (even the Afrikaner himself) the village of Enkeldoorn typifies the narrowest of Afrikanerdom, the nadir of tolerance, the ultimate Siberia of the intellect.

The clash between Afrikaner and Englishman has always been present in Rhodesian white society and politics. Clements points out that the 1922 referendum vote for "responsible government" was just as much an expression of anti-Afrikaner feeling and a wish to avoid involvement in South Africa as a wish to remain British. It is a fact that after 1922, the British connection grew closer and more amiable, and that until the advent of the Rhodesian Front, the whole trend of Rhodesian white society was to dissociate itself from the excesses which have brought South Africa to its current position at the nadir of world regard.

Not that this did the Rhodesian African much good.

CHAPTER THREE

Two Sides of the Coin

Any African nationalist from Rhodesia will tell you with obvious sincerity that his race has been fighting for its freedom ever since the white man came. This is just not true, except in the most obscure psychological sense. After the Mashona Rebellion had been subdued, the white man settled in as the master and the African settled down as the servant. A trusted and liked servant, perhaps, and usually not a slave, but still a servant. The arrogance of the white Rhodesian and the servility of the black between the wars is no doubt galling to the moralist and shame-making to the nationalist, but they were facts of the time just the same.

There is no doubt that any sign of African militancy would have been stamped out as ruthlessly in the 1930s as it was to be in the '60s, but the necessity just did not arise. It was not until the Second World War had partially lifted the veil from African eyes by ending Rhodesia's virtual isolation that the first stirrings of a genuine nationalism made themselves felt.

Rhodesia, so far as Britain was concerned, was solid as a rock for 60 years — an uncomplaining partner in peacetime who demanded little attention and no troops or money, and a wartime ally who could be relied upon at the heart of a valuable continent to keep the peace and to supply men and materials for the battle. Even in the Boer War Rhodesia plumped for the British side, albeit with some misgivings, and there was no doubt where her feelings lay in both the wars against Germany. Nearly 6,000 volunteers joined the British forces during the First World War from a white population of about 25,000, and in the Second World War compulsion had to be used to *prevent* Europeans joining up and to keep them on the land. About 6,500 white men served outside Rhodesia during 1939-45, many of them becoming officers in the Allied forces. Not so widely known, and certainly not so widely publicised, is that double that number of Africans did so too, the majority of them serving on garrison and lines of communication duties.

The impact of a wider world upon thousands of young and impressionable Africans cannot be under-estimated. For the first time they came into contact with new peoples, new cultures. For the first time they were meeting white men on equal terms, and much to their own surprise, finding themselves no less brave, no less competent and no less able to cope with the strains of life than the European. For the first time for them the artificial curtain of white superiority was lifted. Not only did they see American negro officers and NCOs in action, performing the same duties as the white officers, but they found that in other parts of the world the white man himself had to perform the menial tasks. Spud-bashing is the same the whole world over, for black and white. And they found that courage, too, was not the prerogative of the European, who could cower under fire and sweat in terror as well as any African.

The bitterest lesson was inevitably on coming home. For Rhodesia, land of opportunity fit for heroes to live in, was fine if you were a white hero. You received land and adulation and roads were named after you. If you were a black hero, you were lucky if they gave you a job polishing the Prime Minister's car, or standing outside the Post Office with a cane, directing the human traffic into its segregated streams; whites to this counter, madam; blacks to that queue, filthy scum.

The war had other effects upon Rhodesia, too. Not only did thousands of her sons of all races go abroad; Rhodesia, tucked away safely in mid-Africa, became the training centre for thousands of young RAF recruits, who were sent to Thornhill near Gwelo in the centre of the country to learn how to fly, far from the fighting fronts. Inevitably they brought with them the free-and-easy habits of their home life. For the first time, within Rhodesia itself, both white and black Rhodesians underwent the experience of Africans — particularly servants — being treated as equals. The fascination was mutal. Many young fliers, captivated by the climate and the easy way of life, returned to Rhodesia after the war to settle down permanently.

For the first time, Rhodesia began to be taken seriously as an agricultural producing country. Millions of Allied soldiers will recall cursing the Naafi issue of "Sunripe" cigarettes, with their strong raw taste. They were made from the fine Rhodesian Virginia tobacco which was to rival America's within a few years after the war. For the first time, too, secondary industry began to become established within the country, providing the base from which the tremendous post-war boom took off.

In spite of the broadening of Rhodesia's contacts with the world, the country on the surface at least remained as cut off from the main stream of world opinion as it had always been. So far as everyday living was concerned, the war's only effect was to bring about the rationing of petrol. Rhodesia did not so much withdraw from the world of the 1940s (the conscious act which she performed with UDI in the '60s). It was more that the world pulled away, leaving Rhodesia trailing behind in outlook and opinions. No-one was worried. Rhodesia, sleeping in the midday sun, was content to let the world go by.

But the yeast of change was at work, fermenting the brew.

Several elements together gave momentum to the changes which took place in Central Africa after the war. The end of the British Empire in India and the establishment of the separate countries of India and Pakistan set in motion the inevitable counter-current of African nationalism across the entire continent. The influx of Anglo-Indians provided white Rhodesians with their first hints that all might not be well in the white world, that Britain's legendary power as a protector had been drained by two world wars. The need for the white settlers to consolidate their power and their position became apparent to the more percipient of the local politicians. In Southern Rhodesia, as it was then called, the Prime Minister Godfrey Huggins, noting that his country was "a little white island in a sea of black faces", began to make plans to link the white settlers of the high veld with the mineral riches of Northern Rhodesia's Copperbelt. Huggins always argued paternalistically that if you fed an African well enough he wouldn't want the vote; and he sought economic and territorial strength for the white settlers far more energetically than he fought for the myth of political freedom. Always a pragmatist, he was concerned only with the substance of power, not its forms.

Huggins was a successful General Practitioner before he became a politician, and he ran Rhodesia as if it were an outsize practice. The patient was allowed to know just as much as was good for it, and was required to take both medicine and corrective treatment as prescribed. For 25 years, he got away with it. It wasn't a bad run.

After the War, Huggins was faced with a choice. He realised that the special conditions which had led to the wartime boom had ended, and that Rhodesia would have to begin to grow up both economically and politically. The country could either "go it alone" with Dominion status, or it could link up with the countries round it to form some form of powerful economic unit.

There were strong arguments for Dominion status. Certainly on her record of self-government since 1922 and her contributions to the British war effort, she had earned the right to run her own affairs. Had Huggins decided to take this course, there is little doubt that the British Government would have acceded without a struggle.

Whatever reservations the British Labour Party were to have about the advisability of handing over control of between three and four million Africans to a white minority of some 100,000-odd did not appear until later.

Few white Rhodesians felt inclined to go South Africa's way and become another province of the Union, even though, curiously, this was how Rhodesia had been regarded in all forms of sport for many years. The South African way of doing things was rather infra dig for Rhodesians, steeped as they were in the "British tradition". As the New Afrikaner nationalism of Malan and Verwoerd drove South Africa quite willingly along the road to total apartheid, Rhodesians kept themselves aloof and superior. Even the "Dutchmen" in their midst were regarded with something like contempt. First prize in a Rhodesian music hall joke was a week in Enkeldoorn, the Afrikaner stronghold. Second prize, two weeks.

Godfrey Huggins saw very clearly a truth which seems to have escaped Ian Smith and his colleagues now running Rhodesia's affairs. There is little future for a small landlocked country like Rhodesia being squeezed between the jaws of South Africa to the south and the copper economies to the north. Huggins's thinking was largely economic, but he also had a better idea than most what would happen to his country if it were to become the flashpoint of the forthcoming battle between black and white Africa.

After dealing for many years with the quiet diplomacy of the British Colonial Office, which left him to run things very much as he pleased, Huggins believed firmly that he would maintain the same type of control over the reins from the driving seat of the Federation of Central Africa. The economic prospects were dazzling. The initial project was to unite the two Rhodesias, Northern and Southern, allying the strength of the Copperbelt to the growing agricultural and secondary industrial output of the South in one homogeneous whole. The new Federation created in the heart of Africa would counterbalance the growing economic strength of South Africa. Strategically, it would form a strongly pro-Western (more importantly, pro-British) bulwark. And it re-created in some minds at least the dream of Rhodes, the flicker of hope for the "Cape to Cairo" link-up of British interests.

The Colonial Office struck a bargain with Huggins and his fellow-Federationist from Northern Rhodesia, Roy Welensky. They tacked on Nyasaland, long regarded by Whitehall as an economic embarrassment and left to rot in the sun as a Colonial slum. It made very little sense either to Huggins or Welensky to have to take on the liability; but there it was. Either Nyasaland came into the Federation, or there wasn't to be a Federation. In true British style once more, the compromise was adopted and everyone was happy. Except the Africans.

Frank Clements writes: "Whoever supports British traditions has a wide range from which they can select and those chosen by the settlers in Rhodesia certainly included the xenophobia and the arrogance towards coloured peoples, as conspicuous a part of the British heritage as respect for property and the manipulation of the law in defence of privilege. This qualified British patriotism suited the emotions, no less than the purpose of most of the immigrants from South Africa, in number about the equal of those from Britain. They had crossed the Limpopo not so much in protest at the South African policy towards blacks and coloureds as in resentment of Afrikaner policy towards themselves. In Rhodesia they could find the privileges which the Afrikaner was eroding, and they could hope to retain their favoured position by building up the Rhodesian to match the South African power.

"As all the articulate Africans were quick to recognise, Federation, in the years of the majority of whites who supported it, was an attempt to widen the boundaries and to strengthen the forces of white supremacy throughout Africa south of the Equator."

Federation was not sold to Britain or to the world like that, of course. Huggins was much too clever a politician.

Whether he invented the word "partnership" as applied to the relationship between white and black Rhodesians or merely adopted it as a convenient phrase does not matter. "Partnership" became the official policy, implying a hand-in-hand relationship between the races. But words, like statistics, can mean anything you wish. Huggins himself upset a great many applecarts in a rare indiscretion by referring to the partnership of "the horse and the rider," a revealing comparision which delighted the white settlers, but was hardly calculated to reassure the emergent African of his place in the white man's sun. Nor did subsequent statements about "senior" and "junior" partners do much to rectify matters.

There was no doubt that the architects of the Federation fully intended the new alliance to grow into an independent nation, free from the ties of Britain or any other country. In economic terms, the early years of the Federation were an unqualified success. Investment flooded in along with a whole new class of immigrants — managers, insurance men, technicians and that amorphous group which likes to be known as "professionals" — doctors, lawyers, journalists, advertising men, architects; even artists and actors and cinema managers.

The new arrivals brought a new dimension to the staid and self-satisfied white society of Rhodesia. The post-war generation of immigrants came bringing with them the traces of the Left-wing revolution which swept Labour into power in Britain after the war. Some of them indeed, like ourselves, may have been escapees from the drabness of a Britain exhausted after winning the long-drawn-out struggle, but most of them also were fully conscious that that particular war, if it had any merit at all, had been to wipe the racial creeds of Nazism from the face of the earth. Their impact upon Rhodesia was profound indeed, but no less than the impact of Rhodesia upon them.

They found a Federation whose rulers, against political reality, insisted upon and persisted in regarding it as an homogeneous whole. The magnetic attraction of economic success for a short time held the disparate parts of the

Federation as a workable unit. From Britain it looked so good — a strong block of pro-British and pro-Western countries surging ahead into prosperity, welded together by what Welensky once called the concrete wedding band of the Kariba Dam. But a strong economic physique does not necessarily mean the possession of an equally competent political brain, and indeed the Federation from the very beginning contained the seeds of its own destruction.

In the formation of the Federation, it was necessary for the individual units to surrender a great number of the powers and responsibilities they had acquired over the years. These included such vital roles as defence, external affairs, communications and power. But each country was left to administer its own internal affairs much as before, and this included the all-important question of African Affairs.

In fact, Southern Rhodesia had been virtually self-governing since 1923, and what reserved powers the British Government possessed had never been used in any more than a cautionary, consultative capacity. To his death, Lord Malvern, as Huggins became, boasted of his undoubted ability to twist Whitehall round his little finger. So Britain's actual power in Rhodesia had been dissipated over the years until it was virtually non-existent. Southern Rhodesia was ruled by its own Parliament of whites elected on a qualified franchise that was non-racial, but effectively excluded the African by an economic barrier that had been increased through the years with Britain's full assent. With the advent of Federation both the Southern Rhodesia Parliament and its Civil Service remained intact, although weakened by the heavy demands made on both bodies to service the Federal institutions which sprang up.

But in Northern Rhodesia and Nyasaland, which had remained Colonies, Britain retained very real power and responsibility. The two countries' Legislative Assemblies were ruled from Whitehall through appointed "official" members, and Britain's responsibility for the Africans over whom it had assumed power remained both direct and effective, in spite of what the Federationists might have liked to believe. In effect, then, the Africans of the two northern Territories had direct access to Britain and to the House of Commons, while those of the South were still in the same position they had been in since 1923.

Federation was imposed upon the peoples of Central Africa with the best will in the world. But imposed it was. The electorate of Southern Rhodesia voted at a referendum just as they had done in 1922, and decided by more than two to one in favour of the amalgamation. There was no consultation at any time with African opinion, and no attempt either to ascertain or even to form such opinion. In the view of the white Rhodesian an African view-point either did not exist, or if it did, could not count. The white man knew what was best for the African. It is true that Huggins took with him to the London conference two African figures with whom to impress British politicians in London. They were Jasper Savanhu and Joshua Nkomo and they spoke *against* Federation, much to Huggin's disgust. But no-one took much notice of them anyway, and when Nkomo on his return actually stood for a Federal Parliamentary seat, most whites were satisfied that he had been quietly bought off.

It was a curious quirk of fate on that excursion which led to Huggins using his largely forgotten medical skill, possibly for the last time. The airliners of the early 'fifties were unpressurised, and on the return journey the Prime Minister noticed that Nkomo, who is heavily built, was in a very bad way indeed. He immediately diagnosed the trouble and sent for oxygen, thus, he once told me, saving Nkomo's life — "and much gratitude he's shown since," he grumbled.

If the southern Rhodesian whites by-passed African opinion, their indifference was matched by the arrogant assumption of the British political parties (a few Socialists had their misgivings) and the Colonial Office that they knew what was best for the peoples under their care. Such attitudes worked two ways. In the first place, Federation was imposed upon several million people who had no political voice in the decision. On the other hand, because there was no consultation and little attempt was made to persuade the Africans of the advantages that might accrue to them from Federation, to many of them Federation became the symbol of the white man's determination to extend his control over the whole area.

Sir Roy Welensky, the staunchest Federationist of all, still blames the Colonial Office for the failure. He claims, with some justification, that in the fifty years of British occupation of Northern Rhodesia and Nyasaland, the District Officer had, in administering British rule, taken the place of the traditional chiefs of the African tribesman. The District Officer, in his "boma" or administrative centre, had become the guide and mentor, the judge, prosecuting attorney, defence counsel and jury, the wise uncle and the witch doctor for the simple villagers in the bush. If they had a problem, they took it to the D O. If their daughter ran away with a strange man, they sought his counsel. He would adjudicate in cases from the stealing of a chicken to a voodoo murder.

But when Federation was the issue, claims Sir Roy, the Colonial Office failed in its responsibility. The District Officers were told to stand aside, to let the Africans decide for themselves. Because of the directive, the DOs said nothing. When the elders approached them for advice, they remained silent and Welensky believes that from their silence the elders and their followers came to understand that the DO, and hence British authority right up to the Crown, was basically opposed to Federation. He maintains that a positive response would have stilled many of the early fears of the northern Africans and would have given the Federation a chance to spread its benevolent mantle of economic benefits without the political opposition which from small beginnings grew to a crescendo in six years and destroyed the Federation in ten.

In a limited sense, Welensky may be right. But in the broader view, the African intellectuals who first pinpointed the weaknesses of the Federation and of partnership were nearer the truth. Partnership, in spite of the strenuous efforts of the growing number of enthusiastic white liberals and earnest middle-of-the-road Africans in the 'fifties and early 'sixties, never became more than a political slogan. The ten years of Federation brought broad new roads to replace the strips. Cities like Salisbury and Bulawayo mushroomed upwards and outwards with skyscraper office blocks and affluent suburbs. Television arrived to supplement the already competent and all-embracing radio services; and the Kariba Dam harnessed the Zambesi River to spread cheap electricity across the two countries. Africans for the first time sat in the Federal Parliament, and reached Parliamentary Secretary status. An African represented the Federation as High Commissioner in West Africa; and for the first time the big hotels of Salisbury and Bulawayo opened their doors to African customers. With a great flourish, the Federal Parliament de-segregated the Post Office in 1958, five years after the Federation came into being.

But all this was window-dressing which served to conceal the real facts both from the world and from white Rhodesians themselves. The two northern territories, still under Colonial Office rule, were moving by fits and starts towards self-government under a universal franchise, which meant inevitable African rule. In Southern Rhodesia, however, the underlying trend of resistance to liberalism was growing, in direct parallel with the growth in strength and vociferousness of the African nationalist movement. *In practice, every political step made by Southern Rhodesia since the fateful day in 1957, when Garfield Todd was ousted as the territorial Prime Minister, has been further to the Right.*
This was the first political event to make anything like a major impact upon the consciousness of the Parker family, which up until then had been exclusively occupied in settling itself into its new country and becoming accustomed to and absorbed by that strange phenomenon about which the world has heard so much — the Rhodesian Way of Life.

To the outside world, this is usually synthesized into a mental picture of drinks round a palm-shaded swimming pool, two cars per family and meek black servants clad in white uniforms, bowing slightly from the waist. Our first few years could not have been further from this ideal. Our philosophy at the time could have been expressed as: "It's easier to be poor in a warm country than a cold one."

After our idyllic introduction to Bulawayo, we were forced by financial stringency to move into Queens Park, which could be generally described as the "poor white" part of the city. For the princely outlay of £9 per month we were able to rent from the Municipality a bare two-bedroomed house made of pressed mud and breeze blocks. It had a cold concrete floor throughout and a leaky corrugated-iron roof. In the wet weather the tropical storms dripped through the roof into buckets and basins all over the house, and the rain accumulated in a flood outside the kitchen door which was dammed with sandbags. The garden, or "yard" as they call it in Central Africa, was a full third of an acre of red mud which steadfastly refused to grow even kikuyu grass, and contained a bleak thorn tree at the front and a mopani tree at the back. We were separated from our neighbours by a rubber-plant hedge whose thick white sap, we were solemnly assured, was poisonous to children — "Blind him if it goes in his eyes." A wind blew hot and wet from the Zambesi during the summer, and bitterly cold and dry from the Kalahari during the winter.

The Rhodesian Printing and Publishing Company, my new employers, have a fatalistic and long-suffering (and surprisingly good-natured) policy of baling out impoverished journalistic immigrants, and thanks to the general manager of the *Bulawayo Chronicle*, Dave Meggitt, we were able to survive the first few years without actually going bankrupt or landing in a debtors' prison. We accepted gratefully, only coming to realise later that this was all part of the policy of the survival of the whitest which had become the natural law in Rhodesia.

Like most of our fellow-immigrants,we accepted without

demur the white man's criteria for life. We bought a second-hand car, an ancient Hillman Minx which only continual attention kept from the scrapheap. The public transport of both Bulawayo and Salisbury is conceived primarily to take the African to and from his place of work, and the needs of the poor white are of marginal interest. You are not expected to be a poor white in Rhodesia, which has not yet really accepted what white South Africa has known for years, namely, that it *is* possible for a European to be surpassed by an African.

In spite of our comparative poverty, we continued to employ African servants. I like to think that we did not go through the stages usually ascribed to New Rhodesians by the old hands — excessive familiarity, a hit-them-first harshness and brutality, and finally the off-hand, reasonably fair but totally paternal relationship which the average white Rhodesian believes is tolerance and the correct way of "dealing with the Kaffir." But there is no doubt that it took us many years to understand at least partially the real significance of the Rhodesian master-servant relationship.

The old-time Rhodesian and his children regard the African as a conquered people who exist to serve the white settler and his family in whatever capacity the settler likes to choose. It may be in the home, on the farm, in the factory — or even in the Civil Service or police force. Except in very few instances (Sir Robert Tredgold, the former Attorney-General, is an honourable case in point) the Old Rhodesian either fails or refuses to admit the possibility that an African could ever be an equal to a white in any sphere. Should the African step above his station, he must be put down by whatever means are at hand — by word of mouth, shouting, bullying, striking, kicking, whipping or shooting if necessary.

The latter-day settler has a different rationale. His wider background forbids him at least consciously to accept the ideal of the master-race, but this in some ways makes him more dangerous. For he realises, particularly if he is an artisan, that the African is not only capable of, but willing and able to take on the job that the settler is doing; and because of the vastly different standards of living between black and white, the African may well be able to produce the same article at half or even the quarter the cost of white labour. So fear for his position becomes the driving force which dictates that he must keep the African as his inferior in all circumstances. But there is more than fear.

Both for the African and for the European, particularly the European housewife, the master-servant relationship is the point of the most frequent contact between the races. It is almost invariably the first contact particularly for the new immigrant. The housewife from Surbiton or Bexley-heath, transplanted into a strange environment and without experience of employing anyone other than an occasional daily help, suddenly finds herself with a "cookboy", "houseboy", or "gardenboy" at her every beck and call. From the start she is at the disadvantage of not being able to speak to the servant in his own language, and with the unconscious arrogance her environment encourages, in nine cases out of ten she presumes both that the African will pick up her brand of English and that, even if he does not, he will understand what she means.

The usual form of communication is a mixture of the odd broken English that the white man assumes the African understands, delivered preferably in a tone of command — "the only thing the kaffir understands" — plus a smattering of "kitchen kaffir" or "Fanagalo", the bastard lingua franca of Southern Africa. This is an amalgam of simplified English, Swahili and Afrikaans, "Fanaga-lo" means "Do that thing," and a few examples will give the general idea.

"Fanagalo bucket, Jim." Fill
        Empty that bucket, Jim.
        Clean
        Take away
   (depending on the relevant gesture.)
"Fanagalo potatoes."
      Mash Peel
      Throw out Slice those potatoes.

"Fanagalo broom checha, fanagalo carpets outside and bomba them, fanagalo beds jusnow, fanagalo vegetables mush and puttem onna stove, gahli, gahli mind."

(Sweep the floor quickly take the carpets outside and beat them, make the beds right afterwards, clean the vegetables well and put them on the stove to boil, slowly, slowly, mind.)

Perhaps it is not surprising that the most popular stories at Rhodesian sundowners, as the interminable evening cocktail parties are called, are those retailing the inevitable misunderstandings that arise from such a bald means of communication. They are all told in the first person, and each is greeted with guffaws of admiring laughter as if it is the newest thing since pop music. Like the garden boy, who, left to water the beds while his employers were away, did just that. They returned to find every bed in the house dripping wet. Or the same garden boy, dutifully following instructions not to fail to water the vegetable beds every day, standing manfully in the midst of a tropical thunderstorm, his pathetic hose competing with the fury of the elements.

There is the other side of the coin, which most white Rhodesians, old and new, resolutely fail to spin. In most cases, even now, the domestic sphere is the entry point for thousands upon thousands of peasant Africans into the ways of white society. As his command of English improves, and mastery of European techniques, so the ladder of improvement will be from garden boy to house boy to cook boy. At some stage he is likely to step across into industry, where the pay is much better, the tasks likely to be less menial and the daily humiliating contacts with suspicious and intolerant employers fewer.

However, it is impossible for the average European more than to guess at the impression the young African receives when he treads his first nervous steps along the gravel drive up to the master's house. If he is lucky, he will be taken on, at the princely salary of £2.50 or maybe £3 *a month*. He will also receive his food, a fairly generous handful of the staple Rhodesian diet, mealie-meal, a small loaf of bread, margarine and jam, a ration of sugar and tea and about 1 lb of meat per day. This is the Rhodesian category of cheap meat, regarded as fit only for servants. It is actually sold as "boys' meat" and consists of the shin bones, scrag ends and other off-cuts. Most households buy enough for the dogs as well.

Our budding garden boy will also receive an iron bed-frame, and a mattress if he's lucky, on which to sleep in the "kia". There will be some means of cooking — an open fire for which he will be expected to scrounge wood, or a paraffin stove for which fuel will be provided. He will get Sunday afternoons off and, if he has a generous master, maybe Wednesday or Thursday afternoons as well. He will not be able to live with his wife or children if he has any (it is against the law) and if he is caught with a girl in his "kia" it is as good as instant dismissal. He has no security of employment, no written contract, no court of appeal. If his boss should beat him more severely than is customary, he may go the police, but in a society geared to serve the white man's needs, he will likely think twice about this. If he behaves himself, he will probably receive an occasional "bonsella" of a cabbage from the garden or a cast-off pair of trousers from the boss's wardrobe.

In return for these benefits of civilisation he is expected to rise at 5.30 a.m., have the shoes, the car and the step (verandah) polished before the master has his breakfast. Then he will work a 14-hour day in the garden with an hour or so off in the heat of the day. He is expected to learn or understand English within a week, otherwise he is dismissed as "stupid", and is expected to master within the same time the bewildering array of complexities that civilisation provides for the sophisticated — the lawn mower, the washing machine, the polisher, the telephone, the electric stove and the lavatory.

He must ride the tricky tightrope between failure to cope with these various problems ("stupid munt") and doing too well, in which case he becomes "too clever by half" and an object of suspicion. Few white Rhodesians will accept without close question an African who speaks good English — in fact, in many people's book this is an adequate reason for never hiring him. Assuming he manages to come through the early test, he will in turn become a "houseboy" with a wage of between £5 and £7 a month and a cheap khaki uniform; and then a "cookboy" at around £8 to £10 a month, the whole process taking three to five years or so.

Given all these conditions, it is apparent that the average African house servant must display considerable depths of character, courage and ability to accomplish the simple things that every European (in the rest of the world as well as in Rhodesia) takes for granted as his right. Like marrying, having children, bringing them up and educating them. It is small wonder that built into the system on both sides is a tacit acceptance that theft and deceit are inevitable; the only immutable rule that which says: "thou shalt not be caught."

Nathan Shamuyarira, a former editor of the *African Daily News,* about which more later, describes the parallel situation which exists in the industrial section:

"Many workers made — and still make — ends meet through a highly organised system of barter known as "tswete". A man who works in a bakery brings back a loaf of bread to his room in the evening, to exchange it for bicycle parts which someone who works in a bicycle shop brings along. Other workers come bearing spanners, pumps, shoes, shirts, groceries, meat straight from the butchers . . .

"Many European employers have watchmen at the gates who search every worker going in or out of the factory. But they cannot cope with the daring ways the employees use to get bread and food for their very survival.

"A young man who works in a sweet factory will borrow from a friend outsize boots, in order to stuff his socks and boots with 2 lbs or more of sweets. One man carries several sheathes of bacon under his vest. Another throws away a half a dozen tins of condensed milk in the dustbin, covering them with rubbish from the floor, and empties the dustbin privately later. A third drops a large piece of meat in the basin of dirty water he is using to scrub the floor. A fourth sticks an expensive fountain pen into a parcel of sugar he is taking home. A fifth removes spanners in the boot of a car just in for servicing. A sixth gives lifts to pedestrians. So it goes on.

"There is frequent laughter in the townships when people relate to each other the ingenious means by which they succeeded in obtaining these goods without arousing suspicion. It requires extraordinary intelligence and cunning to impress upon your employer the illusion that you really are quite stupid, so dumb in fact that he need have no suspicions. Some men known are now so adept that they can casually weigh out ten pounds of sugar *in the presence of* their European supervisor, instead of ten pounds of mealie meal, selling it to a friend who knows where to take it in the evenings. And when the boss goes off to a bar in the afternoons, the "tswete" business becomes brisk."

On the more privileged side of the colour barrier life, as Tony Anthony had predicted in Rhodesia House in London, grew perceptibly easier for us as we tested the Rhodesian social water and found it warm and welcoming. We began to make friends, found schools for our older boys and in our rattling old jalopy began to explore Bulawayo and the countryside around it.

Two factors combine to eliminate from Rhodesian white society most of the class consciousness which exists in most of the more ancient countries of the Western World. The sense of one-ness, of belonging to the "little white island" (the "laager complex") is the prime factor. It is reinforced by the transient nature of the society itself. The white Rhodesian is always on the move, from Bulawayo to Salisbury to Umtali to Johannesburg to London and back again. Maybe this indicates an underlying acceptance of the temporary nature of residence in the country; the white Rhodesian switches job, house, career and even wife at the drop of a hat while at the same time arguing passionately the cause of permanency.

Everyone knows everyone else in such a society, and a journalist of necessity takes part in what is going on around him. Within a few days of arrival I found myself in search of few gossip paragraphs at an entertainment given by the "Londoners Association" in Bulawayo. There was a music-hall atmosphere in the big hall of Bulawayo's Grand Hotel, with tables and drinks and much cockney chatter. The star of the evening was a large lady with a forceful voice and personality, extravagantly dressed in ostrich-feathers and elbow-length black gloves She sang "My Old Man", "Maybe it's Because I'm a Londoner" and other old favourites, and in between she danced with me and insisted on introducing me to everyone in sight. She was Doris Hatty, wife of Southern Rhodesia's Minister of the Treasury, Cyril Hatty, who was later knighted. It wouldn't, I thought at the time and often since, have happened in England.

On another occasion, I was taken on a three-day safari by the Matabeleland Commissioner of Forestry — my first excursion into the real bundu (bush). The country surrounding Bulawayo is unspectacular in the main and for most of the year a uniform brown. We drove north for a hundred miles or so to the Gwaai River area, and suddenly turned left into the thin forest of mahogany trees and scrub. Some ten miles down the sandy track the Land Rover dipped down sharply out of the line of trees. A two-mile-wide valley of lush green grass spread out before us, the track leading like an arrow straight for the trees the other side. The elephant grass closed around the Land Rover, feet above eye level, but not before my host had pointed out a single sloping roof, tucked in the treeline on the other side of the valley.

This was the home and headquarters of a young Forest Ranger, a Rhodesian-born European, who had already been stationed there six years and had a score of times refused promotion in order to stay in the Gwaai station. He, his pretty wife and their tiny baby were the only white people for twenty miles around. Once a month they would load up the Land Rover for a trip to Bulawayo for supplies. Once in three months they would drive 40-odd miles through ill-defined tracks for a drink with a "neighbour".

Each evening they would sit on their stoep overlooking the valley, and treat themselves to an unbelievable spectacle. The Gwaai Valley is the route of the great game migrations which take place between the Wankie area to the north and Bechuanaland to the south and west. Thousands of elephant, buffalo and zebra are constantly on the move in front of the forester's log cabin as the cool of the evening closes in. Lions, antelope, leopards, baboons pass by in never-ending procession a stone's throw away. At dawn the next morning we shot duck down on the marches of the river, passing two prides of lions and a herd of sable antelope within a half a mile of the cabin. For all I know, that forester may be there yet. He was the most contented and least ambitious man I have ever met.

However, much as I enjoyed my own small venture into interior, the truth of the matter is that like most white Rhodesians we preferred on the whole to project the image of the great outdoors from the comparative security of Queens Park West. More than eighty per cent of all Europeans in Rhodesia live in the suburbs of Salisbury and Bulawayo and the lesser towns, where naught is designed for the white man's discomfort.

Within three or four miles (as comparatively poor whites, we were on the outskirts of the town) we had access to two superb public swimming pools, one of Olympic standard, which only closed for the three colder months of the year; there were four major sports clubs, with facilities for cricket, rugby, hockey and tennis; three modern cinemas; three golf clubs of full championship standard; modern supermarkets and huge chain stores; a theatre of repertory size and a civic auditorium that would hold 1,000; and a City Park of impressive proportions and spectacular beauty. There also probably the best museum in southern Africa and (now) nearly the worst television service in the world, which mercifully was not in being when we lived in Bulawayo.

After a year or so, we decided we could afford to move to one of the better areas. We found a pleasant three-bedroomed bungalow around 20 years old standing in its own grounds, which were in a poor state of cultivation. Some repairs were needed and redecoration and, said the agent, the landlord would be along in a week of two to discuss these. We agreed to pay £25 a month, and moved in. One day soon afterwards, I arrived home from work at about teatime to see a black Rover car standing outside the house, its number-plate a prominent FED 1.

Inside, bouncing our latest baby on his knees and listening to Rachmaninoff's Second Piano Concerto, was our new landlord, the Prime Minister of the Federation, Sir Roy Welensky.

Sir Roy was interested, and interesting. He was not, he told us, a rich man, but he could afford to spend, say, £100 on the house to set it to rights. He agreed to pay for the materials, and we offered to do the work. The agent intervened hastily, worried lest we should paint the walls bright red.

"Let 'em have whatever colour they like," said Sir Roy cheerfully, and drove off in FED 1.

Since that day I have counted this bluff, amiable and totally honest man as a friend. Had he been as understanding a politician as he was a landlord, indeed, I suppose the history of Central Africa over the past 15 years or so might have been different, the Federation might have survived and the Rhodesian tragedy, for that is what it will become, need never to have been written. But even then, in 1957 at the height of his power, Welensky must have had some inkling that the forces that were to destroy him were gathering in strength.

In Lusaka, the militant African nationalism of Kenneth Kaunda was beginning to gain momentum. In Zomba, Chipembere and the Chisiza brothers were planning to bring Dr Banda back from his long exile in London; and in Salisbury, the opposing forces of black nationalism and white supremacy were preparing to shrug aside the "partnership" that had brought the Federal idea into being and to head direct for the confrontation which in retrospect seems as inevitable as it was unnecessary.

CHAPTER FOUR

The Best Childhood...?

Garfield Todd's effectiveness as Prime Minister of Southern Rhodesia ended on that day in 1957 when he flew back from his first holiday in five years, to be presented as he stepped on to the tarmac at Salisbury airport with a sheet of foolscap: the resignation of his entire cabinet. He clung on for the next six weeks or so as head of a rump government of a few loyalists and was then annihilated politically by the United Federal Party.

In subsequent years, particularly when Todd's own role has approached the Messianic in its relation to the African nationalist movement, it has become *de rigeur* to state that he was ousted because his cabinet colleagues could not stand his liberal policies. He was going too fast for his time, is the popular theory.

I wonder if this was really so. Garfield Todd was a New Zealand missionary who found both fame and a respectable fortune in Rhodesia. In his manifold activities in the Shabani area he seems to have displayed benevolent paternalism, missionary fervour and an acute business sense. Certainly he had a far more open mind than the majority of his contemporaries in politics, and as a junior member of parliament after the war caught Huggins's eye as one of the few people who either could or cared to argue with the establishment. The piercing blue eyes, the tall figure, the shock of hair and the eloquence of the preacher made Todd stand out from the ruck of his companions, who were in the main dull and inhibited.

Huggins chose him as his successor when the senior members of the establishment "moved up" into Federal politics. Huggins himself acquired the Premiership of the Federation and a peerage as Lord Malvern, and Todd became Prime Minister of Southern Rhodesia, head of what was really intended to be a glorified County Council. As Prime Minister of the territorial Assembly he was almost totally concerned with internal affairs, which included, most importantly, custodianship of African Affairs. The record is plain that Todd was a tough Prime Minister. He had no hesitation in calling out troops to quell strikes in both Wankie and Bulawayo during his four years in control. And little or no progress was made towards the genuine liberalisation of internal policies — a fact which became apparent when the African nationalist revolution, with the minimum of organisation, spread like wildfire through both townships and reserves in the later fifties. It is pretty clear now that the Todd of those days was — as most of us were — a gradualist who believed in the theory of majority rule but could not really see its coming as a matter of practical politics in Rhodesia for as many years in advance as could be comfortable. Only when he was thrust crudely from power by a conspiracy of the old guard was he forced to examine his position both intellectually and emotionally. And only then did he begin to move towards the stand which was to make him the most despised man in European Rhodesia — the white who gave the black man hope.

This is not to question Todd's sincerity as a champion of the African cause; at the very least he has shown a capacity for development far in advance of that of most of his contemporaries and a moral courage which has withstood that most insidious of all martyrdoms — social ostracism. But it is a fact that Sir Edgar Whitehead, who succeeded him as Southern Rhodesia's Prime Minister, in many ways moved farther and faster on the political road towards a universal franchise and majority rule than ever Todd did when he was in power. I am convinced that the basic reason for Todd's downfall lay more in his style of premiership than in his policies. Certainly, as time passed, he found himself more and more at odds with his old-fashioned colleagues. Todd had been left with a job lot of politicans with whom to make a government; Sir Patrick "Ben" Fletcher and his cronies were never among the brightest of Malvern's followers and had been swiftly discarded when it came to dishing out the plum jobs at the more glamorous Federal level. So had many lesser lights of the Southern Rhodesian civil service. In consequence Todd found himself far more *dictating* to both his government and his senior civil servants than *consulting* them, and it must be admitted that this suited his temperament too. But the result was resentment, and when this was fed with the fuel of racial bitterness over some of Todd's more liberal ideas, the result was a cabinet revolt. Todd wanted more and better African schooling; he wanted to integrate Africans more quickly into the growing industrial society on an equal basis; he wanted to broaden the franchise. Most wicked of all to his colleagues, he wanted to repeal the law which permitted a European man to have sexual intercourse with an African woman, but denied a similar right when it concerned an African man and a European woman.

The whole thing came to a head in February 1958, when the United Federal Party held a special congress presided over by Sir Roy Welensky which finally dismissed Todd from the Southern Rhodesian Leadership. Fletcher led the attack, and Todd demolished his arguments with ease. But the "establishment" was busy reacting from the shock of "partnership" actually being implemented, and after a 12-hour debate and two shows of hands finally agreed to oust Todd and to appoint in his stead Sir Edgar Whitehead, at that time the Federal representative in Washington.

Whitehead appeared to be an extraordinary choice as a compromise (Welensky had sent him to America to get rid of him) or as Prime Minister, or as anything else for that matter. He was nearly blind, peering perpetually through thick pebble-glasses which magnified the already heavy cast in his right eye. He could not hear without a hearing aid, which combined with his poor sight gave his audience — and the public — the impression that he was never quite with them. He was perpetually fumbling with a mal-odorous pipe and searching for matches; and he spoke with a monotonous, machine-gun delivery in total contrast to Todd's inspirational oratory. On all significant subjects, Whitehead had no opinions that were known to the public, which remembered him only as a rather disastrous Finance Minister in the early '50s who had tried sacrilegiously to raise the duty on Rhodesian cigarettes. To the Africans, certainly, Whitehead was an unknown figure; to the Europeans, he was a rather bad joke.

In fact, this picture of Whitehead is somewhat unfair, although it was initially confirmed when he attempted to get into parliament at a by-election in Bulawayo and was defeated by a "cowboy" right wing candidate, Jack Payne. Behind the blindness and deafness was an acute brain, particularly in financial matters. He could speak for two hours in a budget debate without a note and never put a foot wrong. He showed considerable political acumen and ability in piloting through the 1961 Southern Rhodesian constitution which, had they decided to use it, gave Africans their first genuine chance of breaking through peacfully to majority rule; and for a time at least he went further along the road to racial equality than ever Garfield Todd had been prepared to travel. But at the same time he was the author of the draconian measure, the Law and Order Maintenance Act, which — virtually unamended — was the rock upon which, later, the Rhodesian Front built its power and its suppression of both black and white opposition. And under his premiership Rhodesian security forces began the reign of intimidation that has since become the hallmark of relations between black and white in Rhodesia.

All this, and much more, lay in the future when in 1958

the Rhodesian Printing and Publishing Company opened a new evening newspaper in Salisbury under the editorship of Rhys Meier. I was moved from Bulawayo to become its news editor.

At the time, it seemed to us all that the company was riding the crest of the wave of prosperity that had come to Central Africa with Federation. We were not to know that the wave had already reached its peak, and that Salisbury's *Evening Standard* was to record the events which would lead up to the failure of the Federation, the eclipse of Welensky and the end of the dream of "partnership." And four years after it was born the newspaper itself was to die. One of Rhodesia's proudest boasts through the years was that since the Mashona Rebellion in 1896 not a single person of any colour had been killed in anger by security forces. The docility and amiability of the African populace was indeed remarkable, and matched by the paternal regard of the European masters. Over the years, tentative efforts had been made by and among Africans to organise themselves to better their conditions and status, but in the main these were confined to restricted groups in the townships. Lack of education, poor communications no doubt played their part, but one is forced to conclude eventually that really there was not much *demand* for reform, however much *need* there might well have been.

Such efforts as were made stayed strictly within the law. Indeed, until the middle 1950s African movements were solely concerned with altering the system from within. The Bantu Voters Association, for example, formed in 1920, stated as its objects:

1. To safeguard the interest of the Bantu people domiciled in Southern Rhodesia
2. To be the medium of expression of representative opinion and to formulate a standard policy on Native Affairs for the guidance of Parliament
3. To endeavour to secure co-operation with the powers that be and all others interested in the advancement of the Bantu peoples without laying an embargo on their way. (Note "powers that be").

The white Rhodesian of the 1920s believed just as firmly as his successor of the '70s that he knew best what was good for the African; and perhaps not suprisingly did little or nothing to foster the growth of such bodies. They withered and died for lack of interest and lack of money. The white Rhodesian conscience was in the efficient care of the Native Affairs Department, which was left to do its work virtually unencumbered by Parliament or even the law itself. There is no doubt that many competent and conscientious men served the Rhodesian Native Affairs Department over the years, and that in the main and within the limits of the curious Victorian Colonial mentality which flourished (and still does) so strongly, they did their best to be just and even generous. There is equally no doubt that the system quite deliberately created the District Commissioner as second only to God in the eyes of the peasant African, only a damn sight closer and possessed of a cane, a sjambok and a revolver at his hip.

It is also true that over the years the Native Affairs Department played its part in keeping the African in his allotted place in the Rhodesian scheme of things, and did precious little to advance the peasants from the backward conditions under which they have lived for centuries. Nathan Shamuyarira, whom I have quoted before, tells the following story of his first visit to the District Commissioner's office in Marandellas. Nathan was 15 at the time (Ye Gods, to think what I was doing at 15: we are about the same age) and had to get his first registration certificate.

"When we turned the corner of the road and saw the huge Native Department office in front of us, my father alighted from his bicycle. As we entered the yard, he removed his hat, ordering me to take my hand out of my pocket, and not to make any noise whatever as we might disturb or anger the Inkosi (lord) in the office. We spoke to the African Head Messenger who knew my father, and after a few words of greeting we were told to sit down.

"Two hours later the Head Messenger told my father he

had informed the Court Inspector, Mr Tutani, of our presence. It was considered a great favour that word had been sent so quickly. It was not unusual to sit outside the office for four days before being attended to. The Head Messenger told my father proudly that, as an Evangelist Preacher of the Methodist Church he knew he had a lot of pastoral work to do, and he would therefore be attended to as early as possible. In the afternoon we were ushered into the office of the Assistant District Commissioner, who ignored my father's greeting and continued to drink his tea. He dialled two telephone numbers — one to a friend, another on business — before lifting his head to ask through an interpreter:

" 'Indeyiko pano?' ('What does *it* want here?' My father could speak English, but this was not allowed. In the DC's office any African was — and still is — described as 'it').

" 'Nkosi ndine mwana wangu anoda chitupa' (I have a son who wants a registration certificate), my father said in a trembling voice. I had never seen him so frightened.

"After a few routine questions, the verdict came:

" 'Ngayiende kunowona Moses' (It should now see Mr Tutani. Although Mr Tutani was an ageing man who had served the government twice the length of time the young man had, he was referred to by his first name. Perhaps he was lucky not to have been called 'It' . . .)"

Shamuyarira's experiences are still shared daily by millions of Africans in Rhodesia. Perhaps the wonder of it all is that he and hundreds like him have managed to slough off such a tradition of subservience, stronger by far than the tribal shibboleths it replaced.

Between the wars, the African trade union movement was born in Rhodesia, and so began the first mass stirrings against the established rule of black by white. The movement threw up leaders like Charles Mzingele, who organised the first May Day parades in Salisbury and ran them for years, earning a name for himself among the whites as a "dangerous communist". His Reformed Industrial and Commercial Union functioned in both Salisbury and Bulawayo for years, bellowing here, pinpricking there, and generally remaining the only thorn in white authority's side. In the context of his time, Mzingele was a courageous man, maintaining his control of the RICU with ruthless efficiency by denouncing would-be rivals at public meetings. He concentrated his efforts on trying to get conditions improved in the sprawling stinking urban areas, and for twenty years his was almost the only African voice Europeans heard or name they had cause to remember.

Mzingele, a dignified old man when I knew him, with crinkly greying hair, was finally rejected by the African militants themselves. Cruelly and unjustly, his house was petrol-bombed and his children intimidated. He himself was denounced at public meetings and his not inconsiderable achievements on behalf of his fellow Africans derided. He always tried to work, like his predecessors, within the existing system.

When in the fifties the wild young men of the City Youth League, Nyandoro, Chikerema, Chisiza, Sithole and a host of others began to challenge authority directly, their first task was to eliminate "Uncle Tom" Mzingele. They chose the very methods he himself had used for twenty years to eradicate opposition among the Africans; and they were instantly successful. Mzingele, shaken and horrified at being denounced in public as a traitor to his kind, became "respectable." He joined those who for years had been calling him a "communist", became a member of the ruling United Federal Party, and sat at Whitehead's right hand during the talks on the 1961 constitution.

A similar type of African leadership, which the whites regarded as "responsible" and "reasonable" and which the Africans themselves came to despise, was also given by the African National Congress, which was re-formed on South African lines after the war. Under the presidency of the late Reverend Thompson Samkange and with the backing of young educated men like journalist Enoch Dumbutshena (who at one time worked for the *Rhodesian Herald*) the ANC had some initial success. It sponsored the only general strike ever in Rhodesia, in 1948, when for the first (and so far, last) time house servants joined their industrial brothers for 48 hours.

One remarkable character, whom I never met but who was at one time a legendary figure in Bulawayo, was a 250-lb giant called Benjamin Burombo, who had come to Bulawayo from Buhera in the early days of the war and made a bit of money selling biscuits in the railway compound. He had mugged up on the law and on trade unionism, and cheerfully fooled authority for the bulk of his working life. It was only Burombo who could accept from the Chief Justice, Sir Hugh Beadle, a public address van and the commission to tour the Bulawayo townships to tell the workers to return to work during the 1948 strike. Burombo toured the streets all right, using the equipment to broadcast the message to the workers: "Stay away!"

Another early member of the ANC was Joshua Nkomo, who had been educated in South Africa and who had begun his career as a social worker with the Rhodesian Railways. Nkomo's skill as a negotiator was often forgotten during the heady days of the early 'sixties, for the 'forties and 'fifties he rapidly made a name for himself in the Railway African Workers Union, the biggest in the country. He became its general secretary and then President of the African TUC. But his involvement in the tasks of the Federation not only disillusioned the man himself but also discredited him in many African eyes, and by the mid-'fifties he had virtually opted out of politics to run an auctioneer's business in Bulawyo.

It took two years for the City Youth League, starting as a civic organisation aimed at improving matters in the Salisbury townships, to establish itself as the first firm opposition to white authority. After eliminating Mzingele as the champion of African rights, the CYL leaders moved on to sterner stuff. In 1956 they organised a highly successful strike against increased bus fares in Salisbury — the first time that the urban Africans were able to witness how effective retaliatory action could be. At the same time they were preparing to challenge the white man's monopoly where it would hurt his dignity most — in the rural areas — and to form a truly national organisation which would link up the various elements in Salisbury and Bulawayo and the rural areas. They started a newspaper, *Chapupu* (Witness), which did much to consolidate their strength. By the middle of 1967 they were ready to challenge the whole process of occupation and the demoralization of the African people. Fittingly enough, they chose Occupation Day, September 12, 1957, as the day to launch the new African National Congress of Rhodesia.

In the context of African nationalism, the aims and objects of the ANC in 1957 were surprisingly moderate. Even in the choice of leader — the mature, genial Nkomo rather than the firebrand James Chikerema or the rumbustious Nyandoro — the ANC demonstrated its reluctance to use genuinely revolutionary methods. The first statement of principles begins "Its aim is the national unity of all the inhabitants of the country in true partnership, regardless of race, colour or creed. It stands for a completely integrated society, equality of opportunity in every sphere, and in the social political and economic advancement of all. It regards these objectives as the essential foundation of that partnership between people of all races, without which there can be no peaceful progress in this country . . ."

But in the context of Rhodesia, such unexceptional aims when put into effect led directly to the clashes which were to follow. The ANC was an immediate success, the word spreading like wildfire through the country that here at last was an organisation genuinely concerned with African interests. The ANC's first target was the omnipotent Native Affairs Department, its all-powerful officials and the legal implements it had to hand — the Land Apportionment Act and above all the Native Land Husbandry Act.

The simple doctrine that civil servants are servants of the people was new to both Africans and Native Commissioners alike; not unnaturally they welcomed it in different ways. To the Department it was a denigration, a lowering of prestige, an insult which could and should not be tolerated. To the Africans the new attitude was the first breath of freedom they had felt on their faces for sixty years. Its scent was intoxicating.

When Whitehead banned the party 18 months after it was formed, he broadcast his reasons for doing so. Among them were "the growing tendency of the movement to incite people in rural as well as urban areas to defy the law," and he said of the leaders:

"One quality they had in common was an ability to incite a crowd to abuse and ridicule all constituted authority, whether chiefs, native commissioners, missionaries, Federal African MPs and many others working for the benefit of the African people."

As Shamuyarira points out: "He refused to see — or else could never admit — that there must have been deep grievances among the rural people for the ANC leaders to have such swift success; that there must have been bad relations between the people and the native commissioners and chiefs for the ANC leaders to have taught the crowds so easily how these officials were objects of ridicule."

The actions of the ANC in Southern Rhodesia coincided with those of the parallel movements in Nyasaland and Northern Rhodesia, aimed at breaking up the Federation. It was no accident that Whitehead's actions against the ANC in Southern Rhodesia, in which he banned the party and arrested or detained between 400 and 500 leaders, were co-ordinated with the Federal government's attempts to control Dr Banda's Malawi Congress Party. For by this time partnership had virtually died and any real prospect of racial co-operation was at an end. Any lingering hopes that liberalism might have retained were extinguished one by one by the events of the next four years.

By the end of 1963 the Federation had been split up, the ANC had given way to the National Democratic Party which in its turn had been proscribed, the events in the Congo had precipitated thousands of European refugees into Salisbury. (The lesson was lost neither upon blacks nor whites.) Whitehead and Sandys had devised the new

Southern Rhodesian Constitution and the Rhodesian Front had come into power.

They were exciting days to be a journalist, with a ringside seat at the making of history, as it were. We on the *Evening Standard* tried to record the events as they happened with the traditional impartiality of the journalist, but in a small community with such vital issues at stake, inevitably we were drawn closer and closer to the action itself until we ourselves became part of it. It was much easier for the "visiting firemen" from Fleet Street or New York or wherever to take the lofty distant view and lecture us on our shortcomings. As well as being journalists we were also settlers and eventually every one of us in one way or another had to make his choice.

Life, however so it seems in retrospect now, was not all politics at the time. My job as a news editor led me into briefings by Macmillan on his "wind of change" tour; into the headquarters of the National Democratic Party two hours before it was banned and its leaders arrested; into rioting thousands and university discussions. It also showed me the building of the Kariba Dam in all its phases, introduced me to Rhodesian theatre and Rhodesian sport, and at the same time allowed me to see — and sample as only a journalist can on his own home ground — the Rhodesian Way of Life, which is basically what all the trouble is about.

Margaret and I have six children, three of them born Rhodesians. It is certainly true to say that had we not lived in the country for eleven years, not only would those three not have been Rhodesians, but they would not have arrived at all. Some of our cruder friends suggest that there was nothing much else to do with our time, but the truth is that the European's life is both rich and cossetted by the availability of plentiful cheap labour. There is always the underlying thought: the more white children the better . . .

My fourth son Paul was the first of our children to be born a Rhodesian. He is now 15, and the other day he was asked to write an essay on his early childhood.

Unprompted, unabridged, this is what he wrote:

"I was lucky as a child, lucky because my father and mother had emigrated in 1955 to Rhodesia where the summer is long, hot and sunny and the winters dry and cool. Rain came in the summer but not too much and Christmas also happened in the summer. This was the setting for my upbringing. I was lucky in another respect as well — I had three bigger brothers and consequently was hardly ever bored.

"I lived in a very large house with four and a half acres around it, two of which were uncultivated and mainly covered by six-foot-high grass. The whole plot was surrounded by evergreen firs interspersed with blue gum trees. I remember we had one big tree by the drive in which we had built five tree houses. We used to love climbing this particular tree.

"We used to climb another one in the back garden too, and one day while we were climbing it we heard the dogs barking at the end of the line of trees. We thought they were barking at the dog next door, a big black mongrel. Gradually they got nearer.

"Suddenly I looked down and saw what they were barking at. I saw the body of a snake moving in the grass. Quite calmly, I said to my brother: 'Hey, Guy, there's a snake down there and it's coming up the tree!'

"Fear was rising all the time and suddenly we panicked and screamed for help. We jumped and ran for safety, and my eldest brother came out and caught Rupert, the youngest, before he hit the ground. The snake turned out to be a python and was caught later in next door's chicken run.

"One thing that was expected was that we should be able to swim at an early age. The public swimming baths were close at hand and entrance was very cheap at one old penny a time. I could swim when I was five and went swimming almost every day except when the pool was closed during winter. Our next door neighbours had a pool, too, in which we could swim at any time. We also played cricket, hockey, football and tennis.

"School was great fun, starting at eight o'clock in the morning and finishing at one when we went home to lunch. Afternoon activities were not compulsory, but I used to go to all of them, and we had homework every day, even at primary school.

"Life was really fantastic. We did not realise how lucky we were until we came back to this country (Britain) owing to political difficulties. I had not a care in the world except to beat my best friend at school work and games. But in fact I was sheltered from many things like the racial problems.

"Rhodesia is really a wild country, but I did not see any of it. But I returned to this country after having the best childhood anyone could have wished for."

There are two significant omissions from Paul's story — the countryside and, much more important, the Africans. Neither were part of his life, except incidentally. Most White Rhodesians prefer to present the image of belonging to the great outdoors, but in fact more than eighty per cent of them live in a sort of super suburbia. We were no exceptions.

For most of our stay in Salisbury, the family lived in a four-bedroomed double-storeyed house planted conveniently exactly five miles from my office. The fact that it was double-storeyed is important, for it meant that we were just that bit superior to the ordinary run of our neighbours. Although in many cases their abodes were more opulent, they were nearly all of the bungalow type. The house, which was owned by a Rhodesian schoolmaster who inherited the land from his pioneer father, was rented to us, unfurnished, for £40 a month — under £10 a week.

The four and a half acres were ringed with a double bank of trees, climbing up to 60ft high. They were thick evergreen cypress and the lovely Australian blue gum (eucalyptus) which in that climate grows at a rate of 15 feet a year and after 20 years is so brittle that it is liable to collapse without warning. Every winter we would cut one down, burning the sweet-smelling logs on the open fireplace in the living room through the cold evenings (how

English could we get?). Our little "estate" contained every type of citrus tree, and in season we ate oranges, grapefruit and tangerines (naartjies) by the bucketful. There were paw-paws too, and mango trees laden every year with more fruit than we could handle. We plucked avocado pears from two trees in the garden, and laced our fruit salad with grenadillas (passion fruit) blueberries, raspberries, logan-berries and the fast-growing Cape gooseberry. Stakes cut from our mulberry trees sprouted and bore fruit the year after they were stuck in the soil; and with careful husbandry we could get three crops of strawberries each year. We grew potatoes the year round, and while we lived there never bought a green vegetable. Beans, peas, carrots, cabbage, cauliflower, cucumbers and tomatoes flourished on a diet of compost taken from the chickens, and we didn't buy any eggs either. We gave the oversized potatoes to the Africans. We only like the sweet small new ones straight from the soil. We planted roses in January and they were flowering by Easter. One bush of "Peace" provided blooms measuring 14 inches across. One of those would decorate a room by itself. I had to take a step ladder to prune our "Princess Elizabeth" 15 feet up, nine months after we had put them in the ground. Provided you watered, the good Rhodesian earth would provide.

Usually, we had two servants, occasionally three. There would be the houseboy, or girl, the garden boy and a piccanin to run the errands, clean the shoes and be general dogsbody. They rarely stayed longer than a year, although one houseboy, Juram, an honest rogue with a huge grin, kept coming back over a period of six or seven years. I think we fired him, or he us, four times. Muhadi, our longest-serving garden boy, was of the Kumalo clan — the descendants of the rulers of the Matabele — and he stayed with us for more than three years. Like any white Rhodesians, we have our supply of servant stories, and I have no doubt that we provided a share the other way. Possibly the saddest was Winnie, the girl who had reached the sixth grade at her mission school out in the bush and who had to work for a year with us in order to save for her next year's education. She wanted to become an English teacher; she had three years to go before getting her diploma.

One day I asked her to get the marmalade. No marmalade, she said. Yes, I said, there's a new pot, No, boss, sorry, boss.

I took her to the larder. The marmalade pot was there, standing prominently by itself, its label towards us. Winnie shook her head. No, she said, that's not the marmalade.

The point was that she could read and write English immaculately out of a book; when the word "marmalade" was surrounded by pictures of oranges and printed in curly script, she couldn't recognise it. She was an intelligent, diligent girl who was working desperately hard to better herself, and then intended to pass on the learning she had acquired to others.

We wondered then at the quality of the life she had led in her home village, as well as the quality of those who had taught those who had taught her. And wondered, too, how her pupils would fare under her tuition. In three years time she would be teaching, and English was her subject.

The servants quarters consisted of the usual "kia", tucked under the trees away behind the orchard out of sight of the main house. Provided there was no trouble we, like most other Europeans, paid little attention to the goings-on, except to make a periodic inspection of the sanitation, cleanliness, and any spare relatives who might happen to be living there. Bedbugs were eliminated by burning all bedding in sight and fumigating the quarters; squatters were sent packing with much shouting and waving of arms. God knows where the poor devils went to. The nearest township was ten miles away on the other side of the city. It was not our concern.

Africa encroached on our suburban laager very little. White ants plagued the woodwork and snakes were a persistent worry. Apart from Paul's python, we shot a five-foot Egyptian banded cobra on the lawn; we were inclined to take extraordinary anti-snake precautions when collecting the eggs in the morning. One morning a rogue baboon terrified the neighbourhood and kept Margaret and the baby indoors. Another afternoon Margaret shot a civet cat out of the trees with an air rifle. It had been raiding the chickens. And on another occasion we were forced to fence round our beautiful roses against the depredations of a wild antelope, whose favourite food was obviously rosebuds. We were advised to shoot it, but we had neither the gun nor the heart. One morning at dawn I surprised it. It looked at me in mild surprise, finished its mouthful unhurriedly, and was gone in a flash, clearing an eight-foot hedge in a bound.

The domestic day was lubricated for Margaret by the servants and the sun. The houseboy and the garden boy meant that the heavy side of the housework was done, leaving her free to plan, to shop and to cook as she pleased. She was able to play tennis or to spend the morning beside a friend's swimming pool. The afternoon she devoted to the boys' activities, particularly swimming. Each of our sons in turn became an expert swimmer, and for eight years in succession the name Parker was engraved on the Victor Ludorum swimming trophy at Alexandra Park Junior School. Nowadays we look out at the greyness of an English summer's day and recall the long hours spent in the Rhodesian sun, which in any case means that there are far fewer clothes to be washed, and they of course can be guaranteed to dry in half an hour on the line in the brilliant heat.

Schooling for our children was never any more of a problem than choosing the school and then finding a house within reasonable distance of it. European schooling in Rhodesia is given a high measure of priority, and ten times the yearly amount is spent on educating a white boy as on an African. Our schools were well-equipped, modern and well-staffed. Parent-Teacher Associations flourished in the certain knowledge that it would be fine for the fête, or the outing, or whatever, and until 1964, when a nominal charge was imposed, schooling was free. In contrast the African has always been forced to pay for his education in

Rhodesia. One pound or so a term does not sound much, but to a man earning maybe £5 a month it is a considerable sum.

So the wonder is not so much that the standard of African education is low, but that so many manage to find the means to educate themselves and their children in any way at all. The need for education and the urge to obtain it are basic driving forces in Rhodesia recognised by both Africans and Europeans alike as the keys to the future. The story of Kufunda College well illustrates the point.

Kufunda was the brainchild of two European women, both well-off, cultured and intelligent, who realised in the late 1950s that their lives had become both intellectually and morally sterile. One was the wife of a doctor, the other of a University professor, and they found that the continual rounds of bridge parties, tennis parties, coffee, sundowners and dinners was, to say the least, a bit of a bore. So they cast around them for some means of helping the community in which they lived. It did not take them long to realise that so far as Salisbury was concerned, it was the African who needed a helping hand.

A closer study convinced them that — in terms of "partnership" which was the Federal ideal — the one area in which there was a great need for development was the commercial field. Few Africans in Rhodesia can write shorthand, mainly because it is a fiendishly difficult subject to teach in what amounts to the "pigeon English" of the average African; the sound values are different. A few more can type, but competently trained African secretaries and book-keepers are a very rare commodity. Berry (short for Berenice) Hammar and Hannah Wolfson thought they could help fill the gap.

Their coffee parties began to take on a purpose. They quite shamelessly used their position in society to "con" support for Kufunda. The American manager of Remington Rand, who produced £2,000 worth of type-writers on the "never-never," hardly knew what hit him. He didn't even ask for a deposit. Cash, equipment and support flowed in; and in 1958 Kufunda College opened with a small flourish in a back room of a hall in Harare. There were 40 pupils, 20 of them policemen sent by the authorities to learn typing. But Kufunda started as a flop. It was found that the standard of African education had left the pupils totally inadquately prepared for a commercial course. "We couldn't teach them to type," said Berry Hammar, "because they couldn't spell and hadn't got the first idea about grammar and syntax. All the time we were going back to basics."

They discovered that the gap that needed bridging was that between the end of African primary education and the acquisition of the skills necessary for advancement in an increasingly sophisticated society. The Rhodesian education system, quite deliberately, was (and is) turning out people of an educational age of nine or ten years old, in British terms. Berry Hammar and Hannah Wolfson, undaunted, had got their teeth into the problem by now and weren't going to let go. Hannah went back to university to obtain the necessary teaching diplomas; Berry redoubled her sundowner parties to raise more cash. They asked Remington Rand to hang on a bit for their repayments.

Kufunda was then reborn, this time a much more ambitious project to give young Africans the chance to progress from primary education standards to the Junior Certificate of Education level, the lowest qualification recognised by Rhodesian employers as having any significance at all. With the help of sympathetic friends in the Southern Rhodesian Ministry of Education, room was found in a derelict school on the edge of the Salisbury industrial area not far from the Harare township, and school commenced.

That first term there were 40 pupils. Three years later the school had increased to 160, and was employing a full-time African teacher to supplement the work of the European volunteers Berry Hammar had persuaded to join her. Not one white woman had drawn a salary, and the achievements were impressive. Kufunda took only pupils for whom there was no room at the state schools; each had to pay £2 a term for books. They achieved an average pass rate of over 75 per cent at the Junior Certificate level, compared with the government school average of under 40. Officials of the Ministry of Education, who had watched the experiment with interest, were impressed enough to include Kufunda in the Ministry's list of authorised schools – a license to educate. It was the only school to continue operating throughout the African schools boycott of 1962, and its name, which is Shona for "Hope", became famous throughout the African townships. More than 850 children applied for the 40 places available in January, 1964.

Perhaps its success led to its undoing, for it was not until stories of its expansion reached the Rhodesian press that the politicians gave any indication that they acknowledged its existence. But soon after Berry Hammar announced in triumph that the six-year debt to Remington Rand had been paid off, Mr Smith's government decided to end Kufunda's development. They did so in a series of unsubtle moves which were typically ruthless and hypocritical.

First, it was "let be known" that complaints had been received from "local residents" about the behaviour of Kufunda pupils. The fact that the area had ceased to be a residential one some forty years before didn't matter. It was variously announced that the old Coloured school premises used by Kufunda were needed for other purposes, were to be demolished, or were to be converted. Finally, Kufunda was ordered to move, but was not allowed to find new premises for itself; by now the "African" school had to be confined to an "African" area. So with a great display of generosity the government offered new classrooms at a township 13 miles from Harare township, where the majority of Kufunda's pupils were drawn, and more than 20 miles from the white suburbs which supplied all its teachers.

For seven years, Kufunda represented hope as it was given by two dedicated European women to hundreds of African children. As an example of paternalistic human-

THE BEST CHILDHOOD . . . ?   75

ism, it takes some beating. It was destroyed by the Rhodesian Front government because they, of all people, knew that the greatest threat to their own privileged position must be the education of the mass of the African people to a standard at which they will be able intellectually as well as emotionally to challenge the concept of the superiority of white over black.

CHAPTER FIVE

Something New in Politics

Sir Roy Welensky's Federation failed because he was unable to understand or appreciate until far too late the real strength of African nationalistic feeling in the two northern territories. Sir Edgar Whitehead's attempt to hold Southern Rhodesia on a middle course between African nationalism and white extremism failed because he tried to be all things to all men. The Constitution he and Duncan Sandys thrashed out in those tense days of 1961 was designed to hold the balance. It promised continued control of the affairs of the country by "responsible" (i.e.: White) people, but it held out some hope to the African that by participating in the running of the country he would first have considerable influence on both parliament and government; it recognised in the process of time an eventual African takeover was inevitable. Whitehead himself, when pushed, put the period at 15 years, and this remark alone was to prove a large part of his undoing.

As far at Whitehead was concerned, the establishment of the two voting rolls, A and B, and the cross-voting provisions meant that never in the future could an extreme white or an extreme black party take over the running of the government. To explain: both voters rolls were completely non-racial — race was not mentioned. But the qualifications, which were considerably higher for the A roll, ensured that A roll voters would be for many years mainly European, and that most Africans would vote on the B roll. Once in parliament there was no distinction between the two rolls' representatives; they all had equal rights as MPs.

So far so good, but the cross-voting provision is more difficult to explain. Every voter had two votes, which he could cast one for the A Roll candidate, the other for the B-roll. However, in an A-roll seat, the B-roll voters could only have 25 per cent effect, and *vice versa*. In other words, if the A-roll votes cast in a B-roll seat numbered more than 25 per cent of the B-roll votes, then the A-roll votes would be devalued to 25 per cent. But up to 25 per cent of each vote would count fully.

Put more simply, each roll could have up to 25 per cent influence on the other roll's seats, and Whitehead argued that full participation by the Africans would ensure that the white extremists could not take over. The state of the poll – there were approximately 90,000 European voters and only 10,000 Africans, under 2,000 of whom were A-roll voters – was the guarantee against the Africans swamping the vote. Even if they were to do so in the future, their influence on the majority of seats would still be limited to 25 per cent. There were 50 A-roll and 15 B-roll seats.

In such an unsophisticated country as Rhodesia, it was a convoluted piece of legislation which not one European in five, let alone one ill-educated African in a hundred, really understood. Yet to work, it required the wholehearted participation of both communities. It laid down for the first time in Rhodesia a basic Bill of Rights, based on the United Nations Charter, and also endeavoured to chart a clear and peaceful course to the eventual transfer of power from white to black.

Opinions differ sharply on the 1961 Constitution. I believe that, imperfect and complicated as it was, it gave the African nationalist leaders their first, last and only chance to take over the country by peaceful means. Had they told their followers to participate in the new

Constitution, Rhodesia's subsequent course would have been totally different. I believe that by now there might well have been the first African government of Rhodesia. Had the Africans responded to the appeals and the drives to enlist them on to the rolls the Rhodesian Front would not have come to power in 1962. Instead, Whitehead's United Federal Party and the Rhodesian Front might well have been evenly matched in the house, with Whitehead keeping control of the government *with the support of the African nationalists*. The Africans would thus have had the power directly to influence the pace of progress towards majority rule. At the same time, the swamping of the B-roll with African voters would have placed continual pressure on a white-dominated government, by demonstrating the basic absurdity and unfairness of such a segregated system.

The African reply is that this type of response would have led to what has happened anyway — a grouping together of the white parties in coalition against the blacks. I do not believe this necessarily would have been so. The movement towards social and political integration was beginning to gather momentum in the early sixties, and a demonstration by the Africans that they were prepared to work within the constitution to change it could have had a profound effect on European attitudes. In the event, the Africans rejected the Constitution outright, letting the Rhodesian Front into power by the front door by alienating many of those Europeans who had believed in moderation. It was a basic political mistake which set African nationalism back in Central Africa for at least 20 years and led directly to the hardening of racial attitudes. The Rhodesian Front Way of Thought dominates the Rhodesian Way of Life as a direct consequence of the African refusal to accept even the small olive branch that was offered.

The late 'fifties and early 'sixties were stimulating times in which to live in Rhodesia. The three streams of energy ran parallel: African nationalism flared into nationwide activity, bringing wild scenes of joy and enthusiam, but trailing clouds of violence and destruction; white liberalism flamed briefly into life and burnt strongly for a year or two, allowing itself to be snuffed out as the iron of white supremacy entered the soul of Rhodesia. We reported it all, impartially as we were able, but with our detachment rapidly eroded by personal experience and contact. We had lives to live as individuals as well as journalists.

I was the only white reporter on the platform on New Year's Day, 1960, when the National Democratic Party, (NDP) was formed to take the place of the African Nationalist Party (ANC) which Whitehead had banned for its activities in the countryside. There were other Europeans there as well — among them Guy Clutton-Brock, who founded Cold Comfort Farm and who was eventually exiled in 1971, and Terence Ranger, the University lecturer who infuriated the whites by his pro-African stance (He was removed by Welensky). I had become acquainted with Reuben Jamela, the head of the African Trade Union Congress, through reporting his activities and the difficulties he had overcome. He invited me on to the platform, and vigorously resisted attempts by his colleagues to get me thrown off. I had to endure some malevolent glances, but I was left in peace.

It was the first time I had seen the latent yearnings of the ordinary African for independence and freedom of expression brought together in articulate understandable form. This was no ill-considered groping in the dark after the unattainable; these people knew what they wanted and knew they could obtain it. To my surprise, the mood was neither belligerent nor conciliatory towards the white man in Rhodesia; merely determined that disparity and unfairness should come to an end. I was particularly impressed by two speakers I had not heard before: Robert Mugabe and Michael Mawema.

Mawema, a small slight man with a quiet voice and a diffident smile, was elected Acting President. Joshua Nkomo was still out of the country following the ban on the ANC some months previously, and Mawema, who had been on a trade union course in Israel, was elected on a

"locum tenens" basis. Nkomo eventually made a triumphal
return to take over the presidency eight months later, but
in the meantime Mawema made a systematic job of laying
the foundations of a powerful party.

He was perhaps not a strong enough personality to lead
the African peoples of Rhodesia to their freedom, but the
work he did in the two years of the NDP's existence
should ensure him an honoured place in their hearts and
memories. I grew to know him quite well, through
clandestine meetings for journalistic purposes at his little
house in Highfield township, and he showed considerable
courage in the face of persistent harassment from the
Rhodesian police and, later, from the gangs of African
thugs which flourished after the split in the African
nationalist ranks. We would sit in the tiny room over a
bare table with glasses of Castle beer and a flickering
candle. The curtains would be down over the windows and
my car would have been left several blocks away;
Mawema's wife kept watch fearfully at the back door. I
don't suppose I was ever in danger from either rival
nationalists or the white police, but these occasional
meetings gave me both a sense of conspiracy and also
useful information about how the nationalist movement
was progressing.

Mawema's great success was to attract African intellectuals into nationalism for the first time. Mugabe, who
made a brilliant and moving speech at the inaugural
meeting, was one of them. He had three university degrees,
and threw up a lucrative teaching post in Ghana to come
home and work full time for African freedom in Rhodesia.
I recall interviewing him and his beautiful Ghanaian wife in
another tiny house in Highfield township, and wondering
what future lay ahead of this gifted, sophisticated man
who had so much to offer to society. At the time of
writing he has been seven years in restriction: without
trial. Where his wife is, I know not. The last I heard of her,
she had refused to leave Rhodesia to return to Ghana; she
wanted to stay near her husband.

Another was Herbert Chitepo, Rhodesia's first African

advocate. Chitepo took a long time publicly to join the cause of nationalism, but he had a brilliant record of defending nationalists against the many charges which were brought against them. I believe it is true that he never lost a case in court; and certainly time and again he embarrassed the British South Africa Police and the Native Affairs Department by his brilliant advocacy. Eventually he became disillusioned by the internal squabblings of the nationalists, and left to become Solicitor-General of the newly formed state of Tanzania; but more latterly still, he returned to assisting ZANU – in – exile in both Dar es Salaam and Lusaka. Chitepo was a man who concealed his emotions, but who rarely concealed his dislike for the press – the European Press in particular. He strongly disapproved of any one of us being in any form of special relationship with the NDP leadership; and on the night before the NDP was banned made plain his utmost hostility and suspicion when I was admitted into the tiny room behind the shop in Highfield which served as their headquarters.

There was Leopold Takawira, who was to die in 1970 in tragic and suspicious circumstances; he had come over from the multi-racial Capricorn Africa Society which dispensed hope, cash and cocktails with impartial liberality at meetings from Makerere University in Uganda to the Jameson Hotel lounge in Salisbury. There was Enos Nkala, of the wide mouth which was always smiling, and of the wild tongue that preached violence and sedition; George Silundika, teacher and researcher, who became publicity secretary and a superb speaker; and the two doctors, Pswarayi and Parirenyetwa.

Parirenyetwa was perhaps the most forceful personality of them all. After Nkomo returned, I remember "Pari" sitting behind Nkomo's shoulder at Press conferences. The large amiable Joshua was rarely a formidable debater, and it was Pari who would inject the whiplash answers, either himself or through Joshua. Nkomo was sometimes willing to be turned aside by the soft question, to allow himself to be distracted by irrelevances. Pari never. You could almost see Nkomo's backbone stiffening as Pari would lean forward, whispering in his ear the telling phrase or the barbed reply. When Parirenyetwa died in a level crossing accident in 1963 it was a loss that the nationalist movement found hard to sustain. They have never believed that Welensky or Whitehead did not engineer the whole accident.

These people, and many others like Joshua and Ruth Chinamano who, until they were restricted, made such a success of the Highfield Community School, gave breadth, depth and stature to the nationalist movement that it had never possessed before. For the first time the African people had an articulate, responsible voice which began to make itself heard immediately. The cry, "One man, One Vote" began to be taken seriously at last.

Only four months after the NDP's foundation the Party was able to send a delegation of five, headed by Mawema, to London to lobby the Conservative Government in opposition to Whitehead's proposals for rapid independence for Southern Rhodesia within the Federation. Whitehead wanted the removal of the "reserved clauses" — the remaining responsibilities which the British Government retained over Southern Rhodesia — mainly concerning external affairs and African interests.

If Sir Edgar had hoped to accomplish independence by stealth, the reasoned case put up by the Africans was instrumental in preventing the British Government from coming to a decision before the Monckton Commission had reported later in 1960 on the future of the Federation. The story of Monckton has been told in full not only in the Commission's own report but in dozens of explanatory volumes. Here it is sufficient to note that despite all Sir Roy Welensky's threats, manoeuvres and pleading, Monckton spelt the death knell of the Federation in unmistakable terms by allowing both discussion of and conclusions on the right of the component territories to secede.

White reaction to the increasing militancy and effectiveness of the NDP was one of both fright and incredulity.

They could not understand or appreciate that the "munt" was capable of meeting and beating the European in diplomatic argument, and they regarded any attempt to do so as impertinent — the more so, of course, if it happened to be successful. But the white masters also understood instinctively the meaning of the thousands of black men and women who began to mass at the political meetings in Harare and Highfield and the townships around Bulawayo and Umtali. They began to feel the reality of African power breathing down their necks.

Whitehead chose a carrot and stick policy, endeavouring to bow to the winds of change so graphically described by Mr Macmillan, the British Prime Minster, on his African Safari. The liberalising measures offered mini-sops to African advancement but at the same time he brought in ever tougher legislation to appease the rumblings from the not-so-silent European minority. Among his "sticks" was the Unlawful Organisations Act, the first piece of Rhodesian legislation under which a defendant was presumed guilty and so had to prove his innocence.

It was this Act and its ham-handed application by the British South Africa Police, as the Rhodesian police force is still called, which led directly to the shattering of Rhodesia's famous record of 60 years of political peace.

On the morning of July 19, 1960 the first of the infamous "dawn raids" took place. The NDP President, Mawema, its secretary, the late Sketchley Samkange and Leopold Takawira, who was at that time chairman of the Harare Branch, were arrested before dawn and charged with belonging to the banned African National Congress. (Later, they were all three cleared of the charges.) Whether this was Whitehead acting in one of his tougher moods or whether the police, who were often simply stupid, acted on their own initiative, I am not sure. There certainly never emerged any good reason for the arrests, which appeared to me then and still do as an early but typical example of deliberate intimidation by the police.

That night a protest meeting was held in Highfield and as it ended a crowd of more than 7,000 Africans, led by

George Silundika and Enos Nkala, marched to the local police station. There they claimed that the morning's arrests had meant that the NDP itself was illegal, and they demanded to speak to the Prime Minister by telephone. They received no answer. After a long wait, they decided to march the eight miles into Salisbury to the Prime Minister's office. They set off at midnight, but were prevented from entering the city by 500 police in riot kit. At 2.30 a.m. a senior police officer came with the message that Sir Edgar would speak to a delegation of the leaders later that morning.

The word spread, and the crowd swelled through the night. At dawn, something like 40,000 to 50,000 Africans stretched out almost in battle array confronting the police riot squads. But the mood, although anxious, was subdued. We Press were able to move freely on the African side, once we had evaded the restrictive lines of police. Despite the tension, the NDP officials were able to keep far better control of the crowd than the police, a fact which did not go unnoticed and which led on many occasions later to acts of deliberate provocation by the police who could then move in to quell the "trouble" that ensued.

Half the African work force in Salisbury failed to turn up for work that morning. It was not a strike, but a spontaneous protest combined with a natural interest in what was going on. I remember Harvey Ward, my chief reporter at the time, and his somewhat hysterical description: "They're marching on the city . . . It's an attack." It was nothing of the sort.

Nkala and Silundika were allowed through the police cordon and actually reached Whitehead's office. There Sir Edgar, incensed at the whole performance, refused to see them. He went on the radio and called out a territorial battalion of white troops; in the afternoon he told parliament that all meetings had been banned in Salisbury townships.

That night 40,000 Africans slept out under the stars, their food being brought in in relays by friends and relatives. The troops camped down, but the restless movement of reinforcements continued all night. Soon after dawn, the police moved in to break up the crowd with tear gas and batons. Land Rovers roared at groups of Africans to break them up and scatter them through the townships, and overhead the helicopters swooped and harassed them. For the first time, the people retaliated with stones. The African Education Department, with sublime idiocy, closed all the schools, and thousands of children flocked on to the streets to join in the excitement.

That morning, 126 people were arrested for illegal assembly; the townships' streets were strewn with broken glass from police cars and the cars of other whites who had been stoned (we carried some hair-raising stories); a bank was broken into, a hotel badly damaged, a post office van overturned and three people were taken to hospital with gunshot wounds.

The next weekend, in parallel riots along Lobengula Street, Bulawayo, 11 Africans were shot dead by police and more than £100,000 damage was caused. There were no white casualties. The newspapers, including ours, carried vivid accounts of police heroism in the face of African provocation.

The ensuing months brought mounting excitement and involvement as Robert Mugabe, who had taken the job of publicity secretary, began to get his youth groups moving. This was the old City Youth League with a vengeance, and the Rhodesian authorities always construed their activities as intimidation. Parties roamed the townships knocking on doors to call out Africans to weekend meetings. One could always hear stories of beating-up and physical violence being threatened; and certainly in the country districts a growing number of violent incidents were reported of attacks against the symbols of authority — the schools, dip-tanks, teachers' houses and government property being burnt down or destroyed.

On the other hand, the NDP leaders, although they strove for membership, using all the publicity arts from demagoguery to the wearing of animal skin hats like

Joshua Nkomo's, rarely preached open violence; and in the townships a sort of give-and-take toughness became almost a matter of routine in such a rough and bustling country. Our European reporters and photographers cheerfully entered riot-torn Highfield again and again and came out sometimes shaken but with never a scratch. One evening one reporter, Jack Watson, returned from Harare with tiny splinters of glass reflecting the light all over his grey and balding head. He had run into a bevy of stone-throwing youngsters who shattered his windscreen; but that was the nearest to actual injury that we came in all that exciting time.

On the day that Joshua Nkomo returned to take over the leadership of the NDP more than 40,000 Africans turned out to bring him to his Highfield home in triumphal procession. I went along with the *Evening Standard's* photographer, Ken Potter, and watched thousands upon thousands of cheerful Africans trooping along the ten miles to the airport, singing and shouting and dancing. The police put on special security precautions, with hundreds of specials (reservists) in riot kit standing by. There was no trouble; under the Youth Leaguers' careful marshalling the huge crowds remained cheerful, and there was never a hint of anything untoward until Nkomo approached Highfield itself.

Suddenly Potter and I heard a commotion in a side street on the outskirts of the township. We drove out of the column and round two blocks to see what was happening. About 100 Youth Leaguers had clashed with some 25 or so Africans who had criticised Nkomo. As we left the car and approached, the 25 broke and ran for cover. They entered a row of small houses, but they had been spotted. In a Keystone Cops sequence, the 100 pursuers charged into the houses behind them. There was a short pause and then, to the accompaniment of yells, shouts, bangs and crashes, the 25 panic-stricken "antis" burst out through the windows and doors and ran straight for Potter and me. We stood still. There was little else we could do; Our car was 100 yards away. With commendable calm, Potter picked up his camera as they ran towards us and knocked off a couple of quick snaps. The group parted and ran round us, leaving us untouched. As they went by a hail of stones and badly-aimed bricks followed them, also missing us, and then, 25 yards behind, came the Youth League, yelling for blood. Once more they parted, running each side of the pair of us and paying us no attention whatsoever. One I knew slightly.

"Go home, man," he advised *en passant,* obviously enjoying every minute of the chase.

Confrontations between NDP youth leaders and the police became *de rigeur,* particularly at the weekends. The big open squares in both Harare and Highfield townships became the scene of many a skirmish. The youngsters made a game of it; Salisbury is not the first town to take to police-baiting as a sport. The boys used to play "touch-last" with the Alsatian dogs the police took to the townships for riot control. They would gather round a young policeman, standing stiffly with his dog on its leash, taunting both of them until they came too close. The policeman suddenly let out the leash; the dog leapt forward, barking and snarling as the boys scattered, laughing and joking. The penalty for the slowest was a sharp nip in the backside; and he got no sympathy.

It was all most good-humoured, but the mood of an African crowd is volatile in the extreme, matching the sudden thunderclouds which gather out of the blue Rhodesian sky. It took very little, in the circumstances of the time, for a laughing, cheering crowd of smiling faces to turn into a mob of sullen menace. But there were also moments at those meetings when the strength of the yearning for freedom would clutch at the heart; when "Isi Komborera Afrika" rolled from thousands of throats out across the darkening veld and the world stood still.

If the African demands had been excessive, like for example the total elimination of the white man from Rhodesia, the extreme reaction of the European minority would have been more understandable. But even the initial basic need of the Africans for recognition as human beings was rejected out of hand as soon as it manifested itself.

The Freedom Sitters' campaign and the Swimming Bath issues were prime examples of European tolerance which wore thin at the slightest pressure. They were designed by the NDP to test the genuineness of European promises to liberalise the social system. It was astonishing to see the extremes of rage which these comparatively minor escapades provoked.

The Freedom Sitters were a group of courageous Africans who set out to assail the inner ramparts of the white laager — the hotels and the bars. Equipped with respectable suits and collars and ties, they walked into whites-only restaurants and bars and asked, politely, to be served. In some cases, they received their beer, drank up quietly, and left, leaving only curious stares behind them. In others, they were ordered to leave by the white proprietors and refused, sitting drinkless until the police arrived to evict them. Then they left, again quietly, in order not to provoke violence. But more often than not, the whites themselves provided the punch-up; an African asking for a drink in a whites-only bar was, they believed, sufficient provocation to violence.

I witnessed the culmination of the campaign, in the fastness of Meikles Long Bar in the centre of Salisbury, where the only African permitted inside for over sixty years had been the man who swept the floor. Four Africans came through the door. Inside, lined up on their stools at the bar or sprawled at the drab tables was Meikles' motley collection of tanned white muscles, khaki shirts and shorts. No-one said anything as the leading African, a tall young man with a wisp of a beard, asked at the bar for four Castle beers.

"I'm sorry, we don't serve Africans in here," he was told by the barmaid, anxiously. "Please leave. We don't want trouble here."

"We don't want trouble either. We just want a drink," replied the Freedom Sitter. The barmaid asked someone to go for the police. The Africans stayed, standing quietly.

Suddenly an elderly European miner, drunker than the

rest, lurched along the counter, holding his glass.

"F . . . off. We don't want any f . . . ing kaffirs in here."

He stabbed the African in the chest with his finger, hard. The African stood still and looked at him.

"We are causing no trouble," he said. "We would like to be served with a drink."

"I'll give you your f . . . ing drink," said the miner. And poured the contents of his glass over the African's head.

Dead silence. The African stood still, upright, beer dripping down his face and soaking through his thin suit, drenching his shirt and tie. Someone offered him a handkerchief, but he waved it away. The miner turned to the rest of the bar.

"What's the matter with you lot?" he asked belligerently. "Let's chuck these bastards out. They don't belong here."

At that moment, the police arrived to prevent bloodshed. The Africans turned and left, still without retaliating, and the weaker spirits flocked round their champion, slapping him on the back and offering him drinks.

This type of incident was repeated time and again over about six weeks, but the campaign had its effect. All of Salisbury's major hotels opened their facilities to Africans after that, even though the Long Bar at Meikles retained its pure-white image.

The swimming baths constituted perhaps a more inflammatory issue, and the running battle went on for many months. A multi-racial group called the Citizens Association challenged swimming baths segregation in the courts; and won its case.

But it took much more than a mere legal process to overthrow a system which had grown up through the years to the point of fanatical belief. The white Rhodesian has an extraordinary block where matters of hygiene are concerned. Throughout his life, he will require the African to perform the most intimate functions for him. African nannies take care of him from birth, even in some cases acting as wet-nurses, changing his nappies, washing and bathing and feeding him. The African will wash his clothes, make his bed, prepare his food, valet him and cosset his every physical demand. If she is a girl, she will very probably be required to sleep with him, for white Rhodesian desires are every bit as universal as any one else's. Yet the average white Rhodesian will throw up his hands in horror if he is required to use the same toilet as an African, or wash his hands in the same bowl or bathe in the same bath.

Perhaps because the average African had neither the time nor the money nor the inclination to use the swimming baths, the whole swimming baths affair eventually petered out for want of fuel; Africans did not bother to put their legally-based rights to the genuine test. But before it did I was delighted for the first time to be able to use my position for the direct purpose of some intimidation of my own.

One of my reporters, on his day off, watched a particularly unpleasant episode at Salisbury Swimming Baths. There were not many people at the pool and he noted with some interest an Indian boy and his sister, aged about eleven and six, splashing around and generally have a great time. This seemed to annoy a European woman watcher, formerly a Rhodesian swimmer herself and a prominent member of the Rhodesian Swimming Association. Peremptorily, she ordered the Indian children to get dressed and clear out. They did so, abashed and frightened, but the next morning they were back again.

This time the woman chose different tactics. She set a bunch of European children on to the Indians, much as if she was "siccing" on a dog.

I have never felt so angry. I gave the reporter the rest of the week off to stay at the swimming pool. With him I sent a photographer. They had a tape recorder and orders to follow the woman wherever she went. Any move she made against the Indians was to be reported, photographed and, if possible, taped. They were not to do so surreptitiously; the more publicly the better.

It worked. The Indians were not molested again.

However, these things were the pinpricks. The real

effect of the growing strength of the NDP was felt at the top — among the politicians. Duncan Sandys, the Secretary for Commonwealth Relations, limped into Salisbury leaning on his stick, and steamrollered through the Constitution, ably seconded by Sir Edgar Whitehead. But for the first time the Africans were there at the conference table as equals; Joshua Nkomo and the Reverend Ndabaninge Sithole sat through the week of talks and it became plain to white Rhodesia that from now on, at least, they would have to take note of African feelings, African desires and African aspirations.

It was perhaps the effect of sitting at the council table for the first time that persuaded both Nkomo and Sithole that the 1961 Constitution could work. Although Nkomo refused to sign the document, he certainly did initial the draft; and even this moderate expression of approval was greeted by Whitehead and the other negotiators as a triumph. But it soon became obvious that in African nationalist terms, Nkomo had made a cardinal blunder. If there was one thing he could not afford to compromise on, it was the demand for universal franchise. Anything less than "one man, one vote" was regarded by any thinking African as a sell-out. And the 1961 Constitution offered very much less than that, however much of an advance it might have been on what had existed before.

Leopold Takawira, who was away in London under-going medical treatment, came hurrying back, first sending a cable to Nkomo demanding uncompromising rejection. Some days later, Nkomo, back-tracking hastily on his premature initials, came flatly out against the whole deal. He was in time to save his political neck within the NDP, but from then on the intellectuals in the movement never really trusted him. Events were moving too fast at the time for one gaffe to have much effect, and Nkomo's next move did much to restore his lost prestige.

In order to test public opinion, Whitehead arranged a referendum on the Constitution, only qualified voters to take part. Nkomo's NDP called for Africans to boycott the referendum and in opposition organised its own unofficial parallel plebiscite. In both cases the question was the same — acceptance or rejection of 1961 Constitution. The difference was that Nkomo's was based on universal franchise.

Not unnaturally, there was a great deal of huffing and puffing on the part of the Europeans at the infernal cheek of Nkomo's mock poll. In the event it all went off in an orderly manner. The offical virtually whites-only referendum scored a two-to-one vote for acceptance of the Constitution with some 66,000 voters taking part (about 60 per cent of those on the rolls) while Nkomo counted nearly 350,000 votes against and a mere handful "for". It was easy for the Europeans to say, as they did, that no credence could be placed upon such figures — "of course the kaffirs will say anything that suits them" — but in fact it appeared to many observers, myself among them, that the NDP put a tremendous amount of organisation and enthusiasm into their effort. The polling booths were quietly and efficiently run and the NDP "police" prevented any incidents or clashes with the authorities. If the final figures were anything like genuine they demonstrated not only a massive "no" vote as an expression of African majority opinion, but also the dramatic effect the acquisition of universal franchise might have on the legal rolls.

It was this type of political effectiveness which so frightened the whites in Rhodesia. Any demonstration of competence in what had been hitherto regarded as exclusively a white field prompted excesses of rage and a growing hatred that expressed itself in ever more repressive legislation and harsher administrative action. Nkomo's success in speaking to the United Nations — he addressed the Trusteeship Committee for non Self-Governing Territories — the increasing activities of the Organisation for African Unity, Tanganyika's gaining of independence, the NDP's growing fleet of Land Rovers and loudspeakers; all these stimulated the European fear of the inevitable. Therefore, basically, any move forward by the Africans had to be reversed, any upsurge put down, any claim denied and any success minimised until it no longer offended the white Rhodesian eye.

Somewhere between 15,000 and 20,000 people attended the last meeting of the NDP at the Cyril Jennings Hall in Highfield on December 3, 1962. Nkomo was by this time claiming a paid-up membership of 250,000 for the party, whose hold on articulate African opinion in the townships and the countryside was by now virtually complete. It was an astonishing success story for an organisation that had not been in existence a mere two years before.

Six days after that meeting, the NDP was banned; the government claiming that this was necessary to quell the increasing intimidation and violence in the rural areas. Nine days later, the Zimbabwe African People's Union (ZAPU) was formed to take its place, with largely the same leadership. ZAPU lasted as a legal party for only nine months before it too was banned and 250 of its leading members restricted by Whitehead, but it has remained as the symbol of African nationalist resistance ever since, despite the emergence of the rival ZANU group. After the rejection of the 1961 Constitution the split was the second basic mistake the nationalist movement made, and once more Joshua Nkomo can be held to be largely responsible.

Nkomo was a likeable man with an amiable temperament, his round and comfortable figure being hardly the stuff of which martyrs are made. That he has subsequently been able to withstand the rigours of more than six years' confinement and monotony in the wilds of Gonakudzingwa points to unexpected reserves of strength and courage. But he has never been a decisive figure, even in restriction, and his name, meaning the Bull, reflects more the character of a Ferdinand than that of the bold and warlike assailant of white privilege.

There were many apocryphal tales going the rounds of Salisbury and Bulawayo through the early 'sixties; it was easy to smear an African leader over the gins-and-tonics of the sundowner stoeps and there were many uncritical ears ready to receive tales of debauchery and high living in faraway places. Whatever the truth of the various rumours which went the rounds at that time, there is no doubt that Nkomo did enjoy the prominence in world affairs into which his role of champion of the Rhodesian African had thrust him; and it is also a brutal truth that he showed an amazing talent for being absent when his presence as a leader was needed most.

In February 1959 he had been busy in Accra and Cairo when Whitehead moved against the ANC, making 500 arrests. He did not return to take over the NDP until unofficial inquiries had assured him that the heat was off — and he would not be arrested. It may have been coincidence that placed him in Dar es Salaam the day the NDP was proscribed and more than £12,000 of equipment confiscated by the government. But it was plain indecision and lack of guts which kept him away when ZAPU in its turn came under the Whitehead axe. He was then in Lusaka, and instead of flying straight back to face restriction with the 250 other leading members of his party he shot off in secret to Mboya in Tanganyika, with some half-baked idea of mounting a "government in exile". It required some heavy bullying from his right-hand men and from Presidents Nyerere and Kaunda to persuade a most reluctant Nkomo to fly back to Salisbury. As Shamuyarira has written, his lack of leadership at that point knocked the props from under the militant young men and led finally to the splitting of the party a year later.

Nkomo was taken off to three months' restriction in his home area south of Bulawayo, and spent the time working out his plans for a "government in exile". Somehow he managed to persuade the rest of the leadership that this would work, and in April 1963 he led a virtual exodus of the leaders to Dar es Salaam. It was a disastrous trip. President Nyerere didn't want ZAPU hanging around at his expense. The Organisation of African Unity regarded the exercise as futile; it would provide money for strong political activity within Southern Rhodesia, but not for the "chicken-in-the-basket warriors", as Kaunda came to call them, living in comfort far away from their home problems. They were told in no uncertain terms to go home and fight. At home, too, splits began to occur in the party throughout the country. Nkomo, it was thought, had done a good job in stirring up international feeling throughout Africa and at the United Nations. Now it was time he confronted the settlers themselves.

By July 1963, the month after the Victoria Falls conference which dissolved the Federation, the executive party had become totally disillusioned with Joshua's leadership; they determined to depose him. But Nkomo had not been politicking around for 15 years without learning a trick or two. He realised his own position had become precarious, so he moved — fast. He had one reliable ally in James Chikerema, who had only recently been released from four years' restriction by the new government of Winston Field.

Chikerema had caught a young messenger for the dissidents, Edson Zvogbo, recently returned from a stint at the United Nations, with a number of letters to people around Salisbury. On July 6 Nkomo, using the information in those letters, denounced eleven people as the "enemies of his movement". They included almost the entire executive and Shamuyarira, the editor of the *Daily News*. It was a shrewd psychological blow, for Nkomo's name was still the magic one so far as the African public was concerned. He put his opponents beyond the pale; those who had spent five years building the name "Nkomo" into something resembling the second Messiah could not in five minutes undo everything they had built. They were forced to form the rival party, ZANU, with the Reverend Ndabaninge Sithole at its head.

The African nationalist movement has still not recovered at the time of writing, eight years afterwards. Through the traumas of UDI, restriction, sanctions and all that has happened since, the movement has remained divided against itself. Obligingly, the government provided ZANU and ZAPU restriction camps, hundreds of miles apart. In Lusaka, Tanzania and London ZAPU and ZANU representatives squabbled over the meagre pickings available to the fight for freedom.

The whites of Rhodesia found unity based on mutual greed and mutual fear; they had everything to lose, and so they banded together to hang on to it. The Africans on the other hand, with everything to gain, dissipated their effort in individual rivalries and the struggle for power at the top of the movement. It is probably Rhodesia's greatest tragedy — for whites as well as for blacks — that an African leader has not so far emerged who can command the respect as well and the attention and the fear of both races. The whites found Nkomo too easy to despise, for in despising him they devalued all the African peoples in Rhodesia. The blacks helped the whites to smash their organisation into tiny pieces at a time when unity above everything else was essential.

It has often occurred to me that the African nationalists have fought on so many losing fronts and never yet discovered the one potent weapon they possess . . . the weight of numbers.

With a population of some five million in the country compared with under 250,000 Europeans — a ratio of some 20 to one — had the Africans discovered their power in any one of the three main fronts — political, economic or military — they would have been in control of Rhodesia today.

Politically, an African invasion of the voters rolls, even on the qualifications demanded in the 1961 Constitution, would have made the holding of the white minority position impossible in a very few years.

Economically, the Africans could bring white Rhodesia to its knees within weeks by withdrawing their labour *en masse* — and the white Rhodesians know it.

Militarily, the minuscule success of the ill-coordinated mini-forces operating from over the Zambian border proves what could be done. A handful of guerrillas have kept a state of emergency in being for over six years in Rhodesia against the vastly more superior and sophisticated white troops and police. Co-ordinated action against the white masters — a real "night of the long knives" — would change the current situation *overnight*.

Two years after we had left Rhodesia, I spent an evening in the company of a senior overseas official of one of the nationalist parties, putting forward this theory in detail. He agreed enthusiastically, and I suggested a simple and practical method of putting it to the test.

It was a time of low fortunes for the nationalists. Their efforts were unsuccessful and their initiative and effectiveness was being challenged from all quarters. In particular, they needed a propaganda success at the very least to counter the sad disillusionment being expressed in all quarters, especially in the OAU. I suggested that isolated acts against the regime were easily dealt with and just as easily hidden from the public eye. A brick through the window of the Prime Minister's office might make a small paragraph in the Rhodesian newspapers but wouldn't have the slightest effect abroad.

I asked him if he could organise, say, 500 Africans in Salisbury. Each would have one large stone in his pocket, and at a prearranged hour on a certain day 500 stones would be tossed through 500 different windows. There would be no follow-up: the culprits would melt into the night. Some might be caught, but the majority would escape. The tinkle of breaking glass would echo round the world on press, radio and television. No one would be hurt, but the message of resistance would be spelt loud at no cost.

He agreed even more enthusiastically.

And six weeks later *one* rock was thrown through *one* window — of Rhodesia House in London. I often wondered if there was any connection . . .

As the African nationalist movement waxed strong through its succession of parties, corresponding shifts of emphasis were taking place among the white rulers of Rhodesia. The liberalism of the 'fifties crumbled under a series of moral and physical defeats and for the first time the hard core of Right-wing supremacist opposition began to organise itself into an effective political force.

The credibility of the old "establishment" of Huggins and Welensky rested upon the success of the Federation. When its prime champion, Welensky, was outmanoeuvred by Whitehall, Lusaka and Zomba, the Federation was split into its component parts and the basic prop of security was knocked from under the European population — by now 200,000 whites. At the same time they watched at first hand what the excesses in the Congo had meant to thousands of white settlers like themselves. Night after long night the planes flew into Salisbury airport bearing white refugees — men, women and children. Salisbury scoured its cupboards for food and clothing for the unfortunate Belgians; at the same time noting that whereas this time Salisbury was the bolt-hole, where would they themselves run should the same thing happen here? There was only South Africa.

Until the election of December 1962, Sir Edgar Whitehead held his party in power by hovering between the iron hand of the Law and Order Maintenance Act and the olive branch of concessions to African advancement. But his compromise policies, which seemed triumphant when the electorate endorsed his Constitutional proposals at the referendum in July '61 by two to one, received a death blow when the Africans opted out of political participation short of "one man, one vote". Seventeen months later the white electors turned on Whitehead and ousted him with a precisely reversed vote — two to one against.

The United Federal Party never recovered. With only 15 of the 50 A-roll seats and the backing (on racial issues at least) of the 15 B-roll seats in the parliament of 65, Whitehead and his dwindling band of followers fought sturdily to stem the tide that had turned so decisively against them. Their cause had been already lost along with the half-chances of the past. By the time Ian Smith felt strong enough, in 1965, to call for "unity" for UDI, the Rhodesia Party, which was what the rump of the UFP had become, was unable even to offer candidates in all the A-roll seats; and the April 1965 election ended with the

Rhodesian Front in possession of all 50 seats.

The speed of the rise of the Rhodesian Front must be difficult to match in political history anywhere. Up to the beginning of the 'fifties opposition to Huggins in Rhodesia was confined to a "lunatic fringe" — left and right. Through that decade various attempts were made to mount a respectable Right-wing opposition, but they failed to jell, and it was not until the Dominion Party of Winston Field acquired a majority of the votes (though not of the seats) in 1959 that the country had had an adequate glimpse of two-party democracy in action.

Winston Field had come from Worcestershire in the 'twenties, and he retained an obstinate dash of apples and pears in both his complexion and his speech. He was to all appearances the complete gentleman-farmer-politician of the Sir Roger de Coverly mould, owning a very large tobacco farm in the Marandellas area and running it, his family and his servants with leisurely paternalism. But he was never really interested in politics, and under his rather dilatory leadership the Dominion Party disintegrated as its predecessors had into a slovenly and discredited opposition.

Therefore it was something of a surprise that Field emerged as the man chosen by the Rhodesian Front to be its first Prime Minister. For the Rhodesian Front was everything that the Dominion Party had never been and the United Federal Party had forgotten how to be — a ruthless, competent political organisation with a simple goal.

The Front was an amalgam of the disparate elements which had struggled in ineffective opposition to the Hugginsbureau for many years. Its main constituents were threefold. The political wing was led by William Harper who had been the territorial leader of the Dominion Party while Field operated in the Federal sphere. Harper was the ice-cold fanatic from India who had refused to allow his party to participate in the 1961 Constitutional talks, but he sat "observing" in the wings waiting to pounce on the carcass like a small blond vulture. Ian Smith, who had resigned as Welensky's Chief Whip in the Federal parliament rather than be associated with that Constitution, had formed the Rhodesia Reform Party to gather together the dissatisfied members of the UFP. He attracted a number of followers in the Federal sphere, notably the quarrelsome John Gaunt, but his group was still-born as it was absorbed in the Rhodesian Front before it had been in existence more than a few months. The third and most powerful section were the men who became known as the "cowboys" — the small but very powerful group of tobacco farmers and beef barons whose money gave the Front its initial impetus and whose motives were brutally straightforward. They saw in the advance of African nationalism the real threat to their position, their lands, their money and their power; and they were prepared to spend vastly to protect themselves. Their leader, who for the first two years or so of Rhodesian Front rule was the de facto president of Rhodesia, was Douglas Collard ("Boss") Lilford, a millionaire farmer whose way with Africans was as celebrated as his considerable fortune.

Lilford was a six-foot five inch lathe of a man, whose leathery hatchet face epitomised the Rhodesian farming scene. One of his more favourite pastimes was to take his house guests hunting for African game poachers with Land Rovers, searchlights and shotguns. He was backed by Fred Alexander, cotton farmer, and George Rudland, a burly rancher from Matabeleland who was prepared to back the Front's initial advertising campaign with a personal cheque for £25,000. Angus Graham, seventh Duke of Montrose and after the Duke of Norfolk Britain's most senior peer, was among the group but Winston Field was only on its fringes. The "cowboys" did not seek political power themselves; they despised parliament and the parliamentarians, and Lilford went to great lengths to keep himself in the background. Both Graham and Rudland eventually became ministers under Field and later Smith, for want of immediately suitable alternatives, but their political inexperience made them both uncomfortable holders of office.

These men were prepared to supply unlimited funds, in Rhodesian terms, to attain their goals. They believed that so long as Britain retained any form of residual responsibility for Rhodesia, the rate of African advancement to political dominance would increase. In order to maintain white supremacy, the ties with Britain would have to be severed; by agreement if possible or by force if necessary. In order to bring this about, they needed to gain the total backing of the white population.

They began cautiously, establishing "cells" throughout the country to canvass recruits at various levels. They found a deep well of support which at the time suprised even themselves, but in retrospect appears inevitable. Whitehead had never been an inspiring leader, and although he presented the concessions won from Britain at the constitutional talks as virtual freedom, he failed conspicuously to persuade even his close supporters that he was telling the truth Welensky equally plainly was losing his battle to retain the Federation, and the future was uncertain. The Rhodesian Front's professed aims were very close to those of the "establishment", but the Front provided the positive leadership that Whitehead and Welensky had let slip.

Untrammelled by any lingering sense of liberalism, they were able to state very clearly their two-fold purpose: independence first and white rule thereafter. To people wearied by years of constitutional crises it was a clear-cut lead. The Rhodesian Front was formed in March 1962 under the nominal leadership of Winston Field and by December was in power.

Although Field gave the Front its initial badge of respectability which was necessary to persuade the public that nothing too drastic would happen under the new regime, the underlying purpose of the party was always clear. From the start the Front was something new in Rhodesian politics, as new in the European field as the NDP had been in the African sphere. For the first time professional political organisers were employed throughout the country; and for the first time too professional propagandists were brought in to ensure that the public got the message.

The Front's methods were crude, effective and reminiscent. They were designed first to whip up the latent white fears of eventual African domination into a frenzy; and then to provide the answer to those fears. Anyone of whatever persuasion or colour who endeavoured to oppose the march of the Front was immediately shouted down. Sincere questioners at political meetings were branded as traitors almost before they opened their mouths. Claques were organised to break up opposing meetings, often by force, and the trend reached a vicious climax in 1965 when three visiting Labour MPs were roughed up in a deliberately inspired brawl in Salisbury's Ambassador Hotel. More frightening still were methods of dealing with opposition at Rhodesian Front meetings themselves. The spectacle of 400 or 500 white "gentlemen" baying for the blood of a dozen or so African students who refused to stand up when Premier Ian Smith came in to the meeting had to be seen to be believed. That such violence became the pattern at political meetings in Rhodesia or that it was deliberately provoked by the party strong men cannot be challenged.

Field was dropped after 17 months; ostensibly because he refused to lead the party and the country into a unilateral declaration of independence, but more probably because Lilford and the "cowboys" now felt it unnecessary to curry favour with a wavering public. In the meantime the Federation had folded without undue fuss, and Field himself had failed at the Victoria Falls dissolution conference to obtain the absolute independence that his party and the white electorate was now demanding.

In his place came Ian Smith. He had been Finance Minister under Field, and his grasp of the subject had impressed many observers even though his political impact had been negligible enough to make his choice as the new leader somewhat surprising.

The propagandists have done much for Ian Smith. From the start he was presented as the strong, moderate leader, the sportsman and the war hero. Within weeks, "Good Old Smittie" was the toast of Rhodesia. Born the son of a Selukwe butcher and farmer, Smith had been educated in Rhodesia, distinguishing himself on the sports field if not in the classroom, and at Cape Town University. In 1941 he joined the RAF and flew Spitfires in the Western Desert and over Italy, the source of much legend. After the war he had returned, complete with plastic surgery as the result of one of his crashes, and had taken to farming and politics in roughly equal proportions. He was known as the dullest speaker in the Federal Assembly until he quit the United Federal Party over the 1961 Constitution; but he had been Welensky's Chief Whip.

Some are born to greatness, some achieve it and others have it thrust upon them, so the saying goes. Ian Smith acquired it by default, as it were. There was no-one else who fitted the cowboys' bill at the time. His chief rival for leadership, William Harper, the architect of most of the Front's political strategy, was not liked; his tongue was too sharp and his hunger for personal power too apparent. Clifford Dupont, the lawyer who became the regime's first "president" was a sick man thought to be near to death (although he has lasted remarkably well since.) Desmond Lardner-Burke, who had leapt from an obscure legal practice in Gwelo to become Minister of "Justice", had hardly mastered his new portfolio; and Lord Graham, who might have like; the job, had nowhere near the necessary intelligence. (When he was Minister of Agriculture, I heard him propose with all seriousness a plan to set up a "new town" of some 40,000 immigrant Greek and Italian peasants in the tsetse fly area of the Zambesi Valley!)

Someone once wrote of David Frost, the television personality: "How does he do it with his *equipment*?" Much the same could be asked of Smith, whose major political assets are a basic stubbornness and an inability to understand, let alone answer, awkward questions. He has never really mastered the art of public speaking, and he remains awkward and embarrassed in front of the television cameras. Even an innocuous question can throw

him out of gear if it is unexpected. His eyes shift to and
fro; he licks his lips drily, and more often than not fails to
answer the point in question at all. This evasion is
accentuated by his dislike of pressmen. His favourite
weapon is a heavy irony ("What Cabinet meeting?" he will
inquire immediately after coming out of a six-hour
session).

A large question-mark lies over his wartime career which
to my knowledge has never been asked publicly. But why
should the propagandists get away with the hero legend
without challenge? Rhodesia had, as has been stated many
times, a fine wartime record, and Smith, as a fighter pilot,
is entitled to his share of that record. But on the face of it,
his own personal efforts were to say the least undistinguished.

He entered the RAF in 1941 as a Pilot Officer, and left
it four years later as a Flight Lieutenant. On his first tour
of duty as a Spitfire pilot in the Western Desert, he crashed
his plane on landing, and was very lucky to survive. No
mention has been made anywhere of any encounter with
the enemy. Later, when the plastic surgeons had patched
up his face, he returned to his squadron, only to crash
some sixty miles behind the Italian lines. It was six months
before he rejoined the Allied forces, and in the meantime,
say his publicists, Smith organised and led a partisan group
against the Germans.

To give him his due, Smith himself has never claimed to
be a hero; he merely lets the record speak for itself. But it
seems remarkable that at a time when personal careers
were advancing with phenomenal speed, a young
Rhodesian officer should spend four years progressing two
small rungs up the RAF's ladder. He belonged to a section
of the Service renowned for its rapid expansion — and for
its generous dishing-out of deserved "gongs." Rhodesia
claimed its fair share of these. Its most-decorated hero,
Johnnie Plagis, a Greek bottle-store proprietor, came back
with a double DSO, a double DFC and the rank of
Wing-Commander. The fact that he now lives at No 1 John
Plagis Avenue, the street named after him, should not be

held against him. Ian Smith received not even a mention in Despatches, a tribute whichever way one likes to look at it, to the modesty either of his claims or of his accomplishments.

It matters not. Whatever stories are told about Smith by future generations of Rhodesian grandchildren (black or white) they will not concern the war. Smith will be a hero or a villain because he led Rhodesia into UDI, as he was put into power to do. The tide of fortune was running at the flood for the Rhodesian Front, and he caught it at its peak.

From the moment he assumed the Premiership things went his way. It was as if circumstances conspired with the Front. Even the much-feared election of the Labour Party to office in Britain in 1964 turned out to be a blessing in disguise for the Front.

In the first place, the division between the African nationalist parties, and the subsequent outbreak of fighting, intimidation and petrol-bombing in the townships of Salisbury and Bulawayo gave the government the opportunity they had been waiting for to move in and detain every one of the nationalist leaders they could find. It was the biggest swoop yet; about 500 were caught in the net and sent off to the remote camps of Gonakudzingwa and Wha Wha. At one stroke the government had stamped out the violence and removed the political leaders from the public eye. It was necessary for the Front that justice was not only not done, but not seen not to be done.

The break-up of the Rhodesian Establishment after the end of the Federation was another factor. The same faces were there; but the public had ceased to believe in them. Welensky tried ill-advisedly to make a come-back, standing with his former Cabinet colleague Sidney Sawyer in simultaneous by-elections in Arundel and Avondale, Salisbury. Welensky called for a new "party of reconciliation", but that was not the mood either for whites or blacks by this time. He fought the election on the one main plank of opposition to a unilateral declaration of independence and was brushed aside by Smith, who went off to London and came back waving a piece of paper that he said meant that a UDI had gone "out of the window for ever." He claimed that he and the British Prime Minister Sir Alec Douglas-Home had made great progress, and had got right away from any thought of a UDI. It wasn't true, of course, but the electorate chose to believe what they wanted to hear, and Welensky's trumpetings were almost totally ignored. He, and Sawyer, lost overwhelmingly and the challenge was over.

From then on, the Smith exercise in brinkmanship was a brilliant success. He held a referendum that same autumn, asking simply if the electorate wanted "independence under the 1961 Constitution." On the surface it was not a loaded question, and yet the longer the campaign went on and the more times Smith denied that he was seeking a mandate for UDI, the more obvious it became that this was precisely what he was aiming for.

It became even more apparent in 1965, when in April Smith went to the country and won all 50 A-roll seats to take complete control of Parliament; which from then on became nothing more than a rubber stamp for the executive's decisions. From that victory onwards, it was not a question of if, but when independence would be declared. Even here circumstances were in Smith's favour.

The only deterrent left was Britain's willingness and power to act to prevent an act of rebellion. This boiled down to the British Government's power to persuade Parliament to send troops; if there were any doubts about Harold Wilson's wishes at the time they were removed by his abortive trip to Salisbury to try to talk the Rhodesian leader out of UDI. But Wilson was powerless, and he knew it. He had a majority of three in the House of Commons and was facing an election. A decision to send troops *might* have set him down in history as the man who saved racial co-operation and common sense in Central Africa, but he knew full well that it *would* have lost Labour the next election. One politician in a thousand might opt for the shaky chance of a future historical accolade in place of certain current advantage. Wilson was not that man. So on

November 15 at 1.15 in the afternoon, Smith's flat voice rolled out on Rhodesian radios, announcing that the deed had been done, and from now on we were on our own.

Even at that stage, he could not make himself clear. Rhys Meier and I listened to the transistor radio in Meier's tiny corner office in the *Sunday Mail*. From the window you could just see the jacarandas of Cecil Square and the roof of the Parliament building. The nasal phrases rolled on, and we looked at each other, trying to interpret what the words meant. Five minutes later, Ivor Benson walked into the building and announced that under the emergency powers granted by the Governor six days before, he was moving in as chief censor. Only then did we comprehend fully that UDI had been declared.

CHAPTER SIX

The Battle for Men's Minds

The Press has always played a major role in the history and development of Rhodesia, right from the day when a pressman, the chairman of the Argus Company of South Africa, Francis Dormer, coined the country's name, Rhodesia. Its particular and peculiar position dates from the earliest days of settlement, when the *Mashonaland and Zambesi Times* was typed and duplicated in a mud hut by a Pioneer journalist named Fairchild (his grandson was for a time a cadet journalist under my instruction on the *Rhodesia Herald*).

Throughout the country's history, the dominating position of the Argus Company, through its subsidiary the Rhodesian Printing and Publishing Company, has given its newspapers a virtual monopoly in Rhodesia. All the country's major newspapers were and still are part of the Argus empire — and attempts to challenge the monopoly have invariably ended in disaster. Even the Rhodesian Front, which on many occasions has considered starting up its own press in order to counter what it considers the propaganda of the *Rhodesia Herald, Sunday Mail* and *Chronicle* of Bulawayo, has faltered in the face of the costs involved.

From the very early days, when the *Rhodesia Herald* was also the Hansard of the country, reproducing the debates in the Assembly days and even weeks after they had happened, these newspapers have been closely identified with the "Establishment". They have also been totally involved with the white population. In fact, the *Evening Standard* was the first Argus newspaper actively to canvass for circulation in the African townships of Salisbury; and although a number of educated Africans perforce read the *Herald* and the other publications in default of reasonable alternatives, it was not until the late 1950s that a real mouthpiece existed for African opinion.

The newspapers of the Rhodesian Printing and Publishing Co. have been criticised for being narrow-minded and parochial. In fact, they maintained a reasonably high journalistic standard, and much lip service has always been paid within the company to the "freedom of the press". It was always the company's boast that it did not dictate to its editors, that they were free to make their own decisions and to go their own way. It was in fact true, although it was equally certain that if an individual could be expected to stray too far from the mildly paternalistic, gradualist politics of the Argus Company he would not get so far as to be appointed editor in the first place. In the early 'sixties the editors of the principal papers made up a pretty fair sample of this policy.

The "national newspaper", the *Rhodesia Herald*, was run by an amiable journalist whose instincts were both conservative and mildly progressive. Colin Cowan's claims to greatness were few, but he scored one remarkable blow for liberal thought by throwing bodily into the fountain of Salisbury's Cecil Square a young white lout who had punched an elderly blind African in the face. Cowan backed Welensky, as did Rhys Meier, the editor of the *Evening Standard*, rather more forcefully. Meier, a formidable little South African with a German-Welsh background reflected in his name, was considerably more liberal in approach than Cowan, and with a tougher mind and a more outspoken pen. He was prepared to go much further than other editors in recognising the claims of African politicians to recognition — if not to immediate power. Three hundred miles away in Bulawayo, Sidney Swadel, a mild-mannered Scot, infuriated the old-fashioned settlers with his forward-looking leaders in the *Bulawayo Chronicle*, but until he ejected the chief censor from his office immediately after UDI he was prepared to do little to force home his opinions. On the other side of the fence, Austin Ferraz, the Editor of the *Sunday Mail* in Salisbury was probably the liveliest journalist of them all. Moreover, he gauged more accurately than any of us the drift of European opinion to the right, and on the eve of his retirement shook both his colleagues in the Argus Company and the public by violently attacking Whitehead for his progressive policies and advising against the acceptance of the 1961 Constitution. He subsequently retired to South Africa, whence he became a significant advisor to Winston Field and Ian Smith on public relations matters, and was instrumental in persuading a Mosleyite propagandist, Ivor Benson, to become the evil genius behind the Rhodesian Front's "battle for the minds of the people".

Cowan died, Ferraz retired and the *Evening Standard* closed down all within a few months of each other in 1962. Meier took over the *Sunday Mail* and Malcolm Smith, who had been assistant editor to Cowan, became editor of the *Rhodesia Herald*. He was the first Rhodesian-born editor of Rhodesia's leading newspaper, having served with the company since he was a boy, with a break for service in the army during the war. As a journalist he was noted for his stubbornness rather than his brilliance, but so far as the Argus company management was concerned, he could be relied upon to take a generally more cautious line politically than the abrasive Rhys Meier or the subtly stinging Swadel. It would have taken a genuine clairvoyant to predict that Malcolm Smith was to become the staunchest opponent of Ian Smith among all the Rhodesian editors.

I was Malcolm Smith's news editor for more than two years, and rarely saw eye to eye with him as a journalist. Eventually he called me in and told me I was to be transferred to the *Sunday Mail*. He was very honest about it.

"If you were in this chair, and I in yours, you would win. But you're not, and you're going." he said. But our professional differences did not prevent him giving me a defiant lunch at the Salisbury Club when he learned I was to be kicked out of the country.

Smith, Meier and Swadel, then, were the leaders of the Rhodesian Press when Ian Smith was preparing for his UDI. They were backed by L.E.A. Slater, a very tough businessman who was then chairman of the Rhodesian Printing and Publishing Company and who was to become Chairman of the Argus Company. His right hand man was the RP and P's managing director, John Hennessy, a much smoother operator who also came from South Africa. I believe that all of them were genuinely concerned with maintaining the freedom of the Press in Rhodesia, so long as it was consistent with good business practice. They took some, but not too many risks in opposing the policies of the Rhodesian Front; and in the main they were content to follow public opinion rather than to lead it. They held out for some years against the very heavy psychological and physical pressures brought to bear against them, but in the end they succumbed. They did not break; they merely stopped fighting.

As for us run-of-the-mill journalists, we were a motley bunch, as are journalists anywhere. Some of us were British like myself, others South African, and a few Rhodesians thrown in. Nearly all of us belonged to the only negotiating body, the Rhodesian Guild of Journalists, which did annual battle with the Argus Company for more money but by and large avoided political issues. As the Company had a virtual monopoly of the field and most of us were also company employees, the negotiations were largely "house" arrangements.

However, we were concerned with the training of journalists particularly of those Africans who worked for the *African Daily News*, the only daily newspaper that was independent of the Argus Company and the only substantial employer of African reporters and sub-editors. We made repeated efforts to attract the African journalists as members, and for one brief spell persuaded many of them to join the Guild. But we were not able effectively to operate on their behalf, and indeed, from their point of view we were much more concerned with the quality of their training (I suppose like most European trade unionists we gave the impression of being more concerned in holding our own position than with the genuine advancement of the African) than with the content of their pay packets.

In those days, the African *Daily News* was run by two South African brothers, Cecil and George Paver, in an attempt to produce a newspaper of the Africans, by the Africans, for the Africans. The *Daily News* produced some remarkable men but never a successful newspaper. Jasper Savanhu, the first African member of Sir Roy Welensky's Federal government, was one of them. Nathan Shamu-yarira, author and teacher, was another. They were brave journalists, and they wrote well but for one reason and another the *Daily News* rarely succeeded. It never made money, and indeed was propped up for some years by a consortium of copper companies at the instigation of Welensky. It was a poor publication, full of technical and journalistic errors, which never had the money to pay for the proper training of its staff, or to pay them the right money when it *had* trained them.

It was one of my contentions at the time that a professionally-produced paper selling at an old penny could have achieved a circulation of 100,000 in Salisbury alone (the *Rhodesia Herald's* was under 50,000) provided it was prepared to speak out for the African people.

From the moment it came into power, the Rhodesian Front had assessed quite cold-bloodedly its chances, and had come to the conclusion that to remain in power it had to fulfil two major objectives:

1. To obtain independence.
2. To maintain and increase white supremacy.

As in any terms Britain would consider these objectives

were incompatible, the only way they could be reconciled was by an illegal act — the unilateral declaration of independence. For the Front to condition the country to accept UDI, it had to subdue totally articulate African resistance and at the same time secure the overwhelming support of the white electorate where the real power lay.

The phrase "battle for men's minds" was a popular one of the early 'sixties and it dominated the thoughts of most of those engaged in the communications industries — the Press, radio, television, advertising and public relations. Certainly at the beginning of its rule the Front made the positive decision that it had to gain control of the mass media.

It was while Winston Field was Prime Minister that all the groundwork was laid for UDI and the policies that followed, and Field raised not a finger to stop it. He did more. He actively encouraged the campaign that was launched immediately to denigrate the Rhodesian Press and bring it into disrepute. The Front was faced with three choices in so far as the European newspapers were concerned. It was never able to understand or to tolerate reasoned opposition, and the mildest of critical leading articles was calculated to send the whole of its hierarchy into something approaching screaming hysteria. Therefore, the Press somehow had to be won over to the side of the politicians. The Front could set up its own newspaper; it could take over the newspapers of the Argus Company by force — nationalisation — or it could destroy the influence of the Press.

Lilford and his friends ruled out nationalisation. It would have made powerful enemies of the Argus Company of South Africa which, although nominally opponents of the South African apartheid regime, nevertheless still wielded huge influence. There was also the prospect of a running battle with the journalists themselves. We might — would, I still like to think in spite of all that happened — really have fought on this issue. And of course many British sympathisers, particularly in the Conservative Party, would have been lost by such a course.

They made a stab or two at running their own newspaper. They poured money into the *Citizen*, a tabloid run by a Greek called Theo. It had survived through the years as a grubby right-wing weekly, hardly to be taken seriously politically or journalistically. The Rhodesian Printing and Publishing Company's newspapers were too much of a habit with the average European; near-saturation circulations in all the main centres proved it to be too powerful a stronghold for even the Front to overrun. And, whether white Rhodesians liked them or not, they were good professional productions.

Instead, the Front opened a two-pronged attack; first to undermine the political credibility of the Rhodesian Press and second to subvert it from within. Both these activities brought them into direct conflict with the Company and also the Guild of Journalists. Inevitably, as I had just become President of the Guild, this meant me.

I do not want to ascribe too much importance to my own role in what happened subsequently. It is rather to illustrate the amazing lengths to which the Front was prepared to go to lay the foundations for its own complete domination of the Rhodesian newspapers. That they were prepared to bribe, threaten, jail and eventually expel a comparative nonentity for minimal resistance to their plans seems to me adequate comment in itself.

The first round in the Front's self-imposed battle with the Press took place in Parliament. True to the British tradition, speeches made in Parliament there are "privileged", which means that they can be reported publicly to the Press without fear of legal repercussions against the speaker. At Winston Field's instigation, or certainly at the least with his acquiescence for he made never a move to stop it, the back-bench members of the Front launched a daily tirade against the Press. The campaign took a little time to gather momentum, but once in their stride there was no stopping them.

The wildest allegations were made, all of them untrue. Daily cries of "traitor" echoed round the chamber. We were accused of printing lies with deliberate intent to blacken the name of Rhodesia, we were alleged to have taken statements out of context in order to "distort." If one of these drivelling attacks was not printed, up the next day would come the complaint of bias, cowardice, and so on. At the same time, a constant stream of letters written by the Front propagandists (or for them) poured into the offices of the *Herald* running down both the newspaper and the individual reporters. Political meetings were provoked into open displays of hostility against reporters. I and several others were spat at, jeered and called "traitor" merely for sitting at the Press desk at a public meeting and taking notes. On one occasion the Minister of Agriculture, Lord Graham, accused a reporter of writing "lies". On giving the mild reply: "I only report what you say, my lord!" he was ejected from the meeting for his insolence.

The pressure went further. One fine reporter, Tony Hawkins, was hauled before the Committee of Privileges and accused of contempt of Parliament merely for trying to question a Minister who wished to avoid him. Hawkins, who was undismayed by such treatment, worked in tandem with our political correspondent, Ken Brokensha. Brokensha was a gentle South African whose quiet pen strove ceaselessly to find the middle way, the non-provocative phrase. The pressure grew too great for him, the target as he saw it for every barb aimed at the newspaper. He also found Malcolm Smith a difficult editor to work for, and seemed to feel a sense of guilt whenever the paper was attacked by the politicians. He realised as clearly as any of us that the campaign was deliberate but he was unable to disregard it; he took every barb as personal to him. One day he walked into the editor's office and resigned. He opted out of the struggle, and retired to the post of a down-table sub-editor, cultivating tomatoes in his spare time on a small-holding 13 miles from Salisbury. I counted him as a staunch friend, but he could never look me in the eye after that.

My first direct brush with the Front occurred in March 1963 at the first annual congress of the Guild of

Journalists at which I took the chair as President. It had always been the custom of the Guild to invite the Prime Minister of the day to open the congress (in Federal times we had a choice and they changed often enough to allow us to ring the changes.)

Winston Field was therefore invited to address the assembled guests. He made an innocuous speech dealing with general matters, not as far as I can recall specifically mentioning the Press or its place in society in any but the vaguest terms; certainly there was no reference to the current campaign his own party members were waging against us. In reply, I offended against the established rules of protocol by attacking my guest, or at least the party of which he was the nominal head.

I accused the Front of running a campaign of denigration of the Rhodesian newspapers from behind the security of the privilege of Parliament; a series of calculated attacks which we were bound to publish and completely powerless to refute in law. I accused them of using the very laws and traditions they professed to be protecting in order to bring the Press into disrepute, in order to create a public climate of opinion in which the people of Rhodesia would accept without challenge the eventual imposition of censorship of the press. I asked Field, as Prime Minister for an assurance that these things were not happening, or if they were, that they would be curbed; and I am afraid I went on a bit about the danger of suppression of the freedom of the press, and how a free press was essential for the preservation of a free society.

Field smiled a thin smile throughout my rather hesitant harangue (unaccustomed as I was to public speaking . . . etc) and at the end of it all said nothing more than: "That wasn't too bad." I had warned him before of my intentions. But the Rhodesian Front ministers who were in the audience were furious and could hardly bring themselves to drink the Guild's sherry at the reception afterwards.

I had a particularly tough time with Mrs John Gaunt, a largely-proportioned lady who was the driving force behind the then Minister for Information. She was annoyed because (she said) I kept looking at her husband during my speech, especially when I had said anything really abusive. I was hard put to it to explain that as her husband was blessed with similar ample proportions to her good self, and that the pair of them occupied the bulk of the front row, it was difficult to look anywhere else; but that in any case if the cap should fit, Mr Gaunt could well wear it.

As a former native commissioner in Northern Rhodesia, John Gaunt had eked out a precarious living as a journalist for some years before the Front adopted him as a parliamentary candidate. He had written (badly) a vitriolic column in the *Sunday Mail* in Salisbury which had been his main source of income, and now he was energetically engaged in destroying his former colleagues' independence. I had little time for him then. I have none still. John Gaunt is dead. Rhodesia is better off without him.

The sequel to this little confrontation was interesting. I had hardly sat down at my desk at the *Rhodesia Herald* on the following Monday morning when Winston Field came on the line personally. "Prime Minister here," he grated, and proceeded to complain bitterly at the alleged "sensationalising" of an incident at a Bulawayo sports meeting at which a bomb had exploded. He had been present and had received an immediate account of the incident from the police, who had withheld any information whatsoever from the *Bulawayo Chronicle*.

"I wish I was replying to your speech today," he said, and rang off. Two minutes later I received another telephone call. This time it was from a friend and former colleague, Eric Shore, who had quit the sports desk of the *Evening Standard* to take up a lucrative career in advertising. Shore handled the Rhodesian Front's advertising campaign and was very well connected with its hierarchy.

"Are you still looking for a new job?" he asked. He was well aware of my financial state, which was always parlous. The RP and P were never generous payers, and just over

£2,000 did not stretch very far when it came to supporting five children. I was always forced to "moonlight", which included corresponding for the Associated Press, *The Times*, various Canadian newspapers and the Mutual Broadcasting System of America.

"Come over this afternoon. I have something that might interest you."

That afternoon was one of the most extraordinary of my life. Shore ushered me into an inner sanctum and introduced me.

"This is Mr Fred Alexander, Chairman of the Rhodesian Front," he said, and left us alone.

I already knew Fred Alexander slightly. His red face, whitish hair, and slightly bumbling air made him appear insignificant, but he and Lilford were the strong men of the Party and what they said, went. It did not take him long to come to the point.

He offered me a job as "Public Relations Advisor to the Rhodesian Front" at a salary of £3,000 a year, plus a free home, a free car of my own choosing and a virtually unlimited expense account. If the job went well, he said, he personally would guarantee that within a year I would be Minister of Information, with a seat in the Rhodesian Cabinet.

I gaped at him.

"We have a job to do here," he said. "We don't give a damn about the Africans, they don't count. We have to get the support of at least eighty per cent of the Europeans in Rhodesia, and then we can do what we want. It is the only way into the future, to keep Rhodesia white. It must be done. We can do it and we believe you can help us."

I gaped again:

"But why me? You know what I said only last Saturday. You know that I don't agree with anything that you are doing. You know that I've been fighting you as hard as I can."

"We know you can do the job we want you to do. I'm sure our little differences can be ironed out," insisted Alexander. "Is it the money?" We'll make it £4,000 a year then."

I still refused to credit what he said: "I know what you want done, and I think I know how to do it. But how much credibility can you give to such an appointment? I couldn't walk into any newspaper office in Rhodesia and tell them I had joined the Front as public relations adviser. They'd laugh me out of the room."

He looked at me.

"You're President of the Rhodesian Guild of Journalists," he said. "Where you go, they'll follow. That's why we want you to join us."

I laughed at him, but I must confess to at least one night's loss of sleep before I finally turned him down. I still hope he was wrong, and that had I taken up the job Rhodesia's journalists *would* have laughed me out of court. But in the years to come my experiences rather depressingly demonstrated that perhaps after all Fred Alexander had been right.

Three months after this abortive interview, the Rhodesian Front appointed as its public relations adviser an acknowledged Fascist, Ivor Benson, thus for the first time publicly demonstrating the ruthless professionalism which they were to use to gain the support of the white populace.

Benson had once been an English journalist, a supporter of Sir Oswald Mosley. For some years he had worked on the *Rand Daily Mail* in Johannesburg, a highly professional publication itself, and his journalistic competence had taken him to the eminence of assistant editor. But he was fired for writing a leading article (in the editor's absence) advocating strongly a visit by Mosley to South Africa. Subsequently he had worked for the South African Information Service, but his chief notoriety sprang from a series of pamphlets he wrote and broadcast over the South African Broadcasting system advocating total warfare on the menace of Communism, which he saw as threatening the whole of the purified white tip of Africa. The broadcasts were of considerable embarrassment to the South African government, for although they followed the official Nationalist Party line, their sentiments were expressed in outrageously fascist terms which were extremely damaging to the official image. There were signs of relief in many South African quarters when the Rhodesian Front took him on, and one South African newspaper even went so far as to suggest that the South African government should offer to pay the Rhodesian Front Benson's reputed £5,000 a year salary in order to keep him out of the country.

Benson looked, and sounded, a little like his ultimate inspiration, Hitler. He was on the short side, with close dark eyes, a pinched-in mouth and a high-pitched voice. At first he was rather reserved in his opinions, but it soon become apparent that his influence on the policies both of the Front as a political party and of the government itself were considerable. He instigated almost immediately a purge of the government Information Service, ridding it off any officials who might be at all politically suspect. Rhodesia's perennial shortage of civil servants meant that there were few competent officials to take the place of those who quit or who were forced out, and this led to some curious appointments. The quality of the government's information service dropped sharply and has never recovered since. Similar purges were subsequently conducted throughout the civil service.

The government, which already ran the radio service on the well-tried and trusted lines laid down by the BBC through a public corporation, stepped in to take full control. The current Board was sacked, to be replaced by Front nominees of impeccable right-wing standing and a conviction that all news broadcasts should be government propaganda. John Parry, the amiable pipe-smoking Director-General of the Rhodesia Broadcasting Corporation, was forced to resign through ill-health, although his health was quite adequate enough for him to take up a position as Director-General of the Malawi Broadcasting Corporation soon afterwards.

John Appleby, who had headed the RBC's news service with great competence for many years, was sacked and forced to leave the country because he could not find another job. Appleby's weekly commentaries had been a pillar of sanity and commonsense in an increasingly frenetic world, and his loss was felt throughout the country, as well as inside the RBC, where the administration of news fell apart and the standards fell away to a point so low as to be laughable. A mathematics master who had never seen the inside of a newspaper, let alone a radio station, was appointed in Appleby's stead.

Worse was to follow. Rhodesia Television, which had been set up in 1960 as an independent body, was taken over directly. The Front government let the shareholders off (my company was a substantial holder of stock) by eschewing outright nationalisation and merely forcing them to dispose of their holdings under the threat. Immediately, television came under the control of the same board as steam radio and the two media's news departments were put under the control of one man.

I knew him quite well. Harvey Ward worked under me at the *Evening Standard* and *Rhodesia Herald* for four years. He was an energetic but unreliable reporter with a vivid imagination which predisposed the facts of a story before they had actually happened. He was known in the Press Club for his oft-repeated verbal exploits which ranged from recovering from an attack of polio in his youth (which happened to be true) to the many times he had punched this kaffir or that munt into submission and a reasonable respect for his white betters.

There was nothing, according to Harvey, in which he had not excelled. He was and still remains a bore and a bully. At the time we knew him he had a Roman Catholic mother-in-law, a Roman Catholic wife and four Roman Catholic children. Harvey was a convert, and like most proselytes he burnt strongly in the faith of his choosing. He found no difficulty in reconciling his new-found beliefs with the basic ideals of apartheid and the rule of the master-race. He was ideal Benson fodder.

Between them they made a formidable pair. The quality of the news on both radio and television was rapidly reduced to the status of government propaganda, and the television public was treated weekly to the spectacle of Harvey Ward, arms outstretched, knuckles white, gripping the edge of a lectern delivering his weekly homily. It had a familiar theme. Anyone not for them was against them. Anyone who was a liberal (the dirtier word) was either a fellow traveller or a Communist (the dirtiest word). If you were a Communist, then you must of course be a traitor. By simple elimination, then anyone who was not a card-carrying paid-up member of the Rhodesian Front was obviously a traitor. Every news bulletin, every current affairs programme was carefully checked for "anti"-propaganda such as objective news; journalists and even professional entertainment broadcasters were screened for "loyalty". Many quit; some hung on because they had nowhere to go.

As far as the public was concerned, the mass media were sewn up, except for the Press, which still, reaching over backwards to present the news fairly and accurately, constantly betrayed a distressing tendency to criticise the Front and its methods. It persisted, for example, in telling the public that Mr Smith and his friends were intent on declaring unilateral independence, and of course that was the last thing that Mr Smith and the Rhodesian Front wanted said in the early days of 1964.

The Press still felt guilty if it did not report that Garfield Todd could draw an audience of 10,000 Africans to a hall in the white heart of Salisbury: so it reported it. The mere printing of such a "subversive" event was "treachery", according to the Front. So was the reporting of the facts of the public political meetings in which Todd's daughter Judy and her multi-racial friends from the University College of Rhodesia were intimidated, threatened and burnt with lighted cigarettes — meetings at which the Prime Minister, Mr Smith, defending his traditional standards, pleaded mildly from the platform: "There they are, standing there. Don't hurt them too much . . ."

Benson and Ward had other methods. Between them they founded the Candour League, a sinister organisation with a direct connection with the supremacist John Birch

Society of the United States. ("Candour" in this context means "white".) Cells were established throughout the white suburbs of Salisbury and nightly private parties were regaled with literature and films preaching the doctrine of white supremacy were shown, accompanied by the more traditional lavish Rhodesian sundowners.

Members from the Information Ministry began to turn up regularly at functions and parties at the remaining "liberal" strongholds, the Press Club and the National Club, in the Ambassador Hotel. Even the Sunday morning get-together after matins at Salisbury Cathedral became a target for Special Branch attention, both better and lesser-known informers mixing with the congregation and quaffing tea with biscuits in the sun of the cloisters.

Front supporters were planted in church congregations to walk out noisily should the minister preach a "political" sermon which might criticise the government; school parent-teacher associations were infiltrated and reports prepared on the staff. Out-of-line teachers would find their road to promotion blocked; headmasters seeking money for development slipped down the queue; advertisements were withdrawn from the newspapers (although this hardly worked as there were no alternative outlets). The Candour League and similar organisations brought pressure in every sphere of activity — social, economic, political and sporting. Some of it was very successful.

The Communist bogey, inherited as it was from South Africa's politicians, formed a continuous basso profundo to all the Front's propaganda. Every right-wing politician from Smith to Van der Byl, who took over Information, hammered upon the same theme. Basically there was little difference between the policies of the Front and those of the white opposition, splintered though they might be. The Europeans were committed to gaining independence for Rhodesia; everyone stood for the maintenance of so-called "civilised standards" and so far as the advancement of the African people was concerned the only difference was one of pace — "between slow and stop" as one of my African friends put it. But the Front at least, had a message.

Neither the Front speakers nor their listeners would have recognised a Communist if they had met one in the street, let alone would they have understood the difference between the Chinese and Russian brands of the product. Yet Communism was the convenient bogeyman against which everyone had to be on their guard. Communism, it appeared, inspired every action with which they found fault: communism was behind Mau Mau, Kenneth Kaunda, Dr Banda, the Congo situation, Union Miniére, Frelimo, the Argus Company and the Rhodesian Guild of Journalists. You name it, the reds had it.

Ironically, the result of this flood of propaganda has been to create the very situation which they feared. Where no Communist influence existed or was likely to do so, the floodgates were opened. In their struggle to rid themselves of white supremacy, the blacks of Africa were forced to turn to the reds for help and, unlike Britain and the United States, so far Russia and China have not been found wanting.

So now the Chinese communists in their thousands build trans-Continental railways; African leaders cross the sea to Peking and Moscow for training in guerrilla warfare; Russian grenades and Chinese machine-guns are found in arms caches in Salisbury and elsewhere. None of it need have happened.

Probably Benson's major coup was the closing down of the African *Daily News* in August 1964. In the previous few months this newspaper had undergone a face-lift and had shown a remarkable resurgence. The paper had been taken over by the Thomson organisation and, under the new management, had changed both its style and its policies.

The Paver Brothers had always baulked at the first hurdles; they refused to recognise that African nationalism was a force to be reckoned with or that the African public demanded a quality product. The Thomson Organisation put in one of the most accomplished journalists in Central Africa, Eugene Wason, to revolutionise the whole newspaper. Instead of allowing the African journalists on the staff to feed off each other's mistakes, Wason introduced Fleet Street-trained European journalists both to weed out the weaklings and to stimulate the rest. At the same time and for the first time, he aimed the paper directly at the hundreds of thousands of Africans who had flocked to the banner of nationalism. Put bluntly, for commerical reasons he backed Nkomo.

The effect on the Rhodesian public (and upon the politicians) was electric. The circulation of the *Daily News*, years ahead of its time, began to rocket. Blacks and whites both bought it; it was a voice which had to be heard, like it or not. For 18 months Wason and his merry men reported the African scene as it had never been reported before. Even when Joshua Nkomo was sent to Gonakudzingwa, 450 miles away from Salisbury in the bush, Wason spotted a loophole in the law and sent his news editor and a team in a Land Rover to find the detainees. They came back with news and pictures that made the government's measures a laughing-stock. This type of irreverent journalism — Wason even made fun of the chiefs — was too much for the Front.

The day the Government banned the African *Daily News* was a memorable one. The man with the laughable title of Minister of Justice, Desmond Lardner-Burke, had the obviously pleasurable task of telling the Assembly all about it, and outside the Parliament building Judy Todd and 250 university students of all races sat down and protested. They did so in the parking-spaces so as not to interfere with the traffic. One by one they were lifted into Land Rovers and taken away by the police for interrogation. Nothing much happened to them, and they were released later that day. Eventually any charges were dropped due to a technicality.

In the meantime, I was due to debate the "Freedom of the Press" in front of a University audience with Nathan Shamuyarira, a former editor of the *Daily News*, and Ivor Benson himself. It was not an occasion that I had been looking forward to, as Nathan's ability as a debater far outshone my own and Benson's reputation was a formidable one. But the events of the day had put more than fire in my belly and I went into that hall for once ready to take on all-comers. It was an extraordinary evening.

Shamuyarira did not turn up. In his book he describes why; he had got wind of the government's plans to arrest and detain him and he had decided to flee the country. Since then he has not returned to his native land. Ivor Benson did arrive, demonstrating considerable courage in the circumstances.

The lecture hall was packed with students, more than 400 crowding into space normally seating 250. The atmosphere was tense, and Benson was given a thoroughly hostile reception. Judy Todd and her companions were still in custody following the afternoon's events. The university, not unnaturally, was both anxious and angry, and it would have required very little that night to spark a riot. I was not worried for myself, as the audience was wholly on my side, but I had no desire to be present at, least of all seem to officiate at, a lynching.

Benson spoke first. I was disappointed. I had been led to expect polemics of considerable skill. Instead of a toughly-argued case, we were presented with a lecture more suitably addressed to six-year-olds than to university students. I can recall little of what Benson said. Some reference to the dissemination of news like the spread of pollen by the birds and the bees was greeted with growing disbelief; the students could not understand why he refused to talk about the news of the day; surely the closing down of a newspaper was of total relevance to a debate on the "freedom of the Press".

Suddenly, the hall erupted. The students allowed their anger and frustration to get the better of them. Benson's voice rose above the hubbub. Students were on their feet, shouting abuse and gesticulating. I saw a long brown arm shoot out; two eggs sailed through the air, narrowly missing me. One splattered harmlessly on the wall behind us. The other, with an accuracy born of long practice with half-bricks in Highfield, hit Benson squarely on the temple. Its contents ran messily down his face and on to his suit as the audience cheered the marksman to the echo.

We mopped him down, and the chairman somehow restored order. Benson started off again, demonstrating yet again that he had courage, if little common sense. It was as if a switch had clicked in his brain, sending him into top gear. His voice rose two full octaves, and he began his set speech all over again, only this time delivered at twice the pace. He was screaming unintelligibly like a record-player at the wrong speed for what seemed like 15 minutes before audience and chairman combined forced him to sit down. I remembered where I had heard something like it before; recordings of Hitler at the Nuremburg rallies flashed across my mind. He was hustled out of a side entrance before anyone could do him any real harm.

When I spoke, for the first time and the only time in my life I discovered the power of the demagogue. My every argument was listened to in devout silence; every joke I made was greeted with hilarious laughter and every point I thrust home received with rapturous applause. In the middle of it all Judy Todd appeared with her companions, fresh from the Salisbury police cells, and a huge cheer went up. There was little in what I said to stir the heart strings, I am sure; but the occasion was so emotional that I could say nothing wrong.

I remember little of what I did say, but recall receiving a full minute's standing ovation for a single-word answer: "Yes." It was that sort of night, and at least I learned that the difference between a good speech and a bad one may well lie in the ear of the receiver and not the mouth of the deliverer.

But it all made no difference in the long run. The *Daily News* was banned for subversion, and Wason left the country for good. Lord Thomson disappointed us all bitterly by refusing to contest the banning and declining to defend, as we saw it, the true freedom of the Press.

It was our first experience of how genuinely petty in the eyes of the world were the problems of Rhodesia. All that money and all those people's livelihoods; and yet Thomson was defeated without a battle to leave the defence of the freedom of the Press in Rhodesia in the same hands that had always held it — those of the Rhodesian Printing and Publishing Company.

CHAPTER SEVEN

"Unwarranted Persecution"

When in 1967 the Smith regime eventually removed censorship, I wrote an article for the *Guardian* newspaper in London which got me into considerable hot water with Malcolm Smith, who had by then quit his job in the hot seat as Editor of the *Rhodesia Herald* and retired to a leisurely life in London. He was particularly hurt by my allegation that the Rhodesian Press as a whole and individual journalists in particular had done very little to fight for that freedom of the Press about which they so often wrote so movingly in their leading articles.

Malcolm Smith did in fact fight — but not for his right to print the news without fear or favour. He fought for the right to print nothing at all, which I suggest was the wrong battle at the wrong time for the wrong cause. He fought like a tiger to keep the blank spaces in his newspaper caused by the censor's scissors, and to avoid filling up the spaces with other news or leave, as the other newspapers did, "token spaces". But neither he nor any other Rhodesian editor found the courage at any time to print the news the censor had removed, or openly to defy the "laws" by which the regime steadily eroded the prestige and position of the Press.

Malcolm Smith, with considerable courage, did distribute to overseas correspondents galley proofs of his leading articles which the censor had removed, but a visit by the police, the confiscation of the offending "pulls" and the threat of prosecution were enough to put to an end that little caper.

On the sister paper, the *Sunday Mail*, Rhys Meier maintained his stance of grating and lofty disapproval of the regime, and 300 miles away the *Bulawayo Chronicle's* Sydney Swadel physically threw Ivor Benson out of his office; but in fact there was very little they could do to prevent the inevitable happening.

The papers were caught in a vice partly of their own making, and partly well forged for them by Benson. In fact since the honeymoon days of the Federation in the 1950s the papers had steadily drifted away from white Rhodesian public opinion. Smith and his colleagues, and Field before him, often accused the Rhodesian Press of being inconsistent; but in fact the Press stayed faithful to the ideals and principles they had been expressing for 20 years. It was the public which had changed its attitude, and instead of representing and reflecting what its readers had come to feel the Press found itself swimming against a tide of disapproval which quickly turned into a flood.

In mounting any form of defence against the type of attacks which were being made at the time the Press was hoist with its own petard of trying to represent the news fairly. This is what Benson knew and manipulated so well. The Front had no need and indeed no wish to be fair. It was quite ruthless, and day after day we journalists would be forced to swallow our indignation and sit helpless as speech after speech and letter after letter flooded the news columns.

As the pace towards the UDI hotted up, so did the pressure on both the editorial and managerial sections of the industry. The destruction of the *Daily News* had given the Front much courage, and our masters in the head offices in Salisbury and Johannesburg knew they were walking a desperately narrow tightrope. Journalistically and in business terms they were ready to take on any opposition, but they could not fight the power of a government which daily held over their heads the threat of nationalisation or direction of the newspapers by the government. It was in early 1965 that a friendly soul in the Ministry of Information passed on to me anonymously a paper prepared within the ministry on the costs of setting up a rival newspaper, concluding that it would be too expensive and recommending one of the other two courses instead. In the event, neither happened. But censorship did.

It says much for the patience and forbearance of the management that, so far as I am aware, it never departed from the long-standing Argus principle that an editor could be sacked, but not interfered with. I have no doubt many late-night candles were burnt over many anxious discussions, but each editor was left to plough his own furrow (or dig his own grave if he wished). Over the years, with the exception of the brilliant but inconsistent Austin Ferraz, all the editors had followed the roughly similar pro-Welensky line of gradualism. (It was Ferraz's knowledge and understanding of the strengths and weaknesses of the Argus Company and its employees that helped Benson and the Front to exploit them so well). Throughout the whole traumatic period leading up to UDI the act itself was consistently opposed editorially in all the main newspapers. But by this time words were too late. Few members of the public were reading, and certainly only a handful heeding, the warnings issued against UDI not only by the Press but by almost every responsible body of opinion in the country outside parliament.

If there was doubt and concern in the minds of our bosses, there was also confusion among the journalists themselves. As "journalist", like "liberal," became a dirty word in social circles, the cracks began to show in our hitherto united ranks. It was not that newspapermen did not agree with the theory of the freedom of the Press, it was a matter of how far they were prepared to go to defend it. Unfortunately, as in many journalistic enterprises, the gulf between the managerial side and the editorial was a wide one.

The Rhodesian Printing and Publishing Company's attitude towards journalists closely resembled its treatment of its African workmen — paternalistic and distant. Journalists wrote words and provoked trouble; they did not earn income for the firm as did the advertising department, instead they spent it. They could not handle money like the management men, and were always in debt and having to be bailed out. Responsible journalists, maybe. Responsible citizens — well, hardly ever.

It was our experience in the Rhodesian Guild of Journalists that this attitude extended through daily working relations to industrial relations, wage negotiations and conditions of work and employment. The management meant well, but if any idea was presented by us employees, it was instantly suspect and, if possible either ignored completely or shelved to gather dust for future generations.

The fact that the management itself could make mistakes rarely occurred to its eminent members. The impressive new *Rhodesia Herald* building in Cecil Square was found — the day it opened — to have only one w.c. for some 150-odd women employees; and a £6,000 illuminated mural looked fine until the main staircase was placed in front of it, obscuring at least 50 per cent of it from public gaze. More serious was the fact that although several hundreds of thousands of pounds were spent on the building, there was no air conditioning. In consequence in summer when the temperature hovered in the eighties the building was intolerably hot; and in the winter when the winds blew from off the Kalahari it was cold enough in the big open-floor office to necessitate the wearing of an overcoat; conditions that were not alleviated by the knowledge that executives' rooms were provided with individual air conditioning units that blew hot or cold at a touch.

In consequence, in the circumstances which threatened all our livelihoods, there was to be no concerted action between management and the journalists to meet the threat which was obvious to us all. As President of the

Guild of Journalists during the whole period I must accept
as much blame as anyone for this. At our annual wage
negotiations some lip service would be paid by either side
to the necessity to maintain the rights of a free press; but
we never got down to taking concrete steps which could
possibly have had some effect, if only to inject some
backbone into a pretty spineless lot. It must be acknowledged that we had a great deal on our plates at the time,
but there was certainly a basic failure in relationship for
which both sides must share the blame. We just did not
trust each other enough.

The fact that the Rhodesian Printing and Publishing
Company backed me in my own battle with the Rhodesian
government and were willing to pay several thousands of
pounds in my defence perhaps makes these opinions sound
contradictory, not to say ungenerous. But mine was not a
case of the company's choosing. The circumstances were
forced upon them in terms of a newspaper's collective
responsibility for what it does – or does not – publish,
they had little option but to become involved.

Strangely, the only other Rhodesian journalist to go to
jail on an ethical matter, a former editor of the *Bulawayo
Chronicle* called Sydney Veats, had also refused to reveal
to the police a source of information. In his case it was the
writer of a letter who admitted painting a statue of the
great Cecil Rhodes red, way back in the 1930s.

To explain what happened to me and why it all turned
into something of a *cause celèbre* one must have some
understanding of the background. The by-elections in
November 1964, in which Smith destroyed Welensky's
attempt at a comeback with typical ruthlessness, had
convinced the Prime Minister that he had the necessary
European public support for a unilateral declaration of
independence. As his civil service was still in the process of
being purged (it was not until November 1964 that the
head of the Army, Brigadier Jock Anderson, resigned
because he refused to support UDI) there were still
significant gaps in the government's knowledge of the real
ability of the country's economy to withstand the

inevitable effect of sanctions. To fill these gaps and to give some semblance of a public debate on the matter, Smith asked various public bodies to prepare for the government their own independent assessments of the prospects of their different sectors after a UDI. These bodies included the Farmers Union, the Rhodesia Tobacco Association, the Associated Chambers of Commerce and the Association of Industries.

The prognostications, although hedged round with provisos that they were considering only the economic and not the political consequences, were uniformly gloomy, and were certainly not in the style that Smith had wanted. At a time when he was trying to whip up public enthusiasm for a go-it-alone course, it was not helpful for the Tobacco Association, for instance, to forecast accurately enough that a UDI would destroy the industry that provided something like 40 per cent of all the country's overseas earnings.

This particular report was the first to be completed, and it created a furore. Angus Graham, the Duke of Montrose who was at that time Rhodesia's excuse for a Minister of Agriculture, blew his top. He called the authors of the report "traitors" in public, which was a little hard in that his tobacco farmer friends were not only the strongest supporters of the Rhodesian Front but also its main financial prop.

There is no doubt that this report, and the Farmer's Union version that followed it, were considerable shocks for the government. Smith, Benson and the Secretary for Information, Van der Byl, were at this time almost exclusively involved in trying to suppress any adverse information about UDI and to promote its potential advantages. They brought heavy pressure to bear on the remaining bodies not to release their reports for public consumption.

Of these the two most important were the Rhodesian Chambers of Commerce (ACCOR) and the Association of Rhodesian Industries (ARNI) whose analyses were awaited with increasing interest. As the days went by and the reports remained private speculation mounted both as to their content and tone. We in the Press considered the documents to be of vital importance to the public, and hammered away at the task of getting them released. There was also, one must admit, the vicarious thrill of getting a "scoop" if one could secure first publication.

One Friday in January 1965 I received a telephone call from an old and valued "contact" who invited me to go to his office immediately. He had "something of interest" to show me. I arrived to find that he had acquired, I know not how, photostat copies of both the outstanding reports. Because of the touchiness of the situation, and because the documents had been "side-marked" with comments in a handwriting that might have been recognisable, he stipulated that I could not take them away. I was allowed to make what notes I liked on the spot and, if I found myself able to use the story, I was not allowed to quote directly from the documents. I agreed, and studied them for two hours.

The analyses showed that both the Chamber of Commerce and the Association of Industries were wholeheartedly opposed to a UDI on economic grounds, but like their colleagues in farming they hastened to make it clear that this was an economic judgment; they left the assessment of the political consequences to the politicians. Nevertheless, they were "hot" documents which added a good deal of fuel to the fires of the anti-UDI faction in the country, and given the political circumstances and attitudes of Smith and the Rhodesian Front, it was understandable that the government wished to delay publication as long as possible.

With my notes burning a hole in my pocket, I hastened back to the office and wrote my report. Mindful of my promise to my source, I did not quote directly. The story was full of journalistically defensive phrases like "it is understood that" and "reliable sources say that" but nevertheless it gave the full gist of both reports and it was pretty obvious that whoever had written it must have had access to the reports themselves.

At this time I was working as chief sub-editor on the *Sunday Mail;* our publication day was the following Sunday. I showed my report to the editor, Rhys Meier, and he agreed that we should run it in full. It was a natural "lead story" in the circumstances prevailing at the time. He had one reservation, however. He wanted to be absolutely sure in his mind that the documents I had seen were genuine. The issue was one fraught with so many consequences, particularly in view of the government's reaction to the publication of the previous documents, that he was worried lest the *Sunday Mail* was being "used" to plant a bogus story on the public. He suggested, and I agreed, that the next morning we should submit my report to the bodies concerned and ask for their comments.

The next morning, a Saturday, I did so. I read the report over separately over the telephone to the secretaries of both bodies. We were left in no doubt about the genuineness or accuracy. Within an hour we were informed that if we intended to go ahead with publication the next day, both ACCOR and ARNI would seek a High Court injunction to prohibit publication *on the grounds of infringement of copyright.*

Rhys Meier had no intention of breaking the law. He was meticulously careful, although opposing the UDI policy of the Rhodesian Front to the last ditch, not to place the newspaper for which he was responsible in the position of being accused of deliberately flouting legality. The *Sunday Mail* climbed down. We informed ARNI and ACCOR that in the circumstances we would withold publication (under protest) and asked them in return to ensure that when they were ready to release the contents they should do so for first publication in the *Sunday Mail.* And there, we thought, the matter would rest.

Later we learned that on legal advice, ARNI and ACCOR had referred the matter to the Prime Minister's office, and that everything that followed was on the direct instruction of Ian Smith himself. On the Monday, Rhys Meier received a visit from Chief Superintendent May of the Salisbury CID and another senior officer. On the grounds that they were investigating a breach of the Official Secrets Act, they demanded to know (1) who had written the story; and (2) what was his source. Rhys Meier refused to give either piece of information. He maintained — and this was the key to our whole defence — that the documents concerned could not be held to be "official secrets" as they had been prepared by bodies outside the government and concerned a hypothetical situation which had nothing to do with the security of the state.

Chief Superintendent May persisted. He said that if the editor continued to refuse to give information he himself would be liable to prosecution for withholding evidence, and that furthermore he would then be obliged to question each member of the *Sunday Mail's* staff individually. Both sides then adjourned to consider their position.

I was called to a round-table conference with the Managing Director, John Hennessy; the General Manager, David Meggitt; and Rhys Meier. Our attitude was unanimous; our source must be protected at all costs. This was the basic journalistic ethic on which we were all agreed without hesitation. But the matter of how far we would co-operate with the police was another question. Rhys Meier wanted to refuse to give any information whatso-ever, including the name of the person who had written the story. He had the good editor's instinct to protect his staff.

I felt differently. It was one thing for the person in possession of all the facts to refuse to talk; he knew what he was not talking about, as it were. On the other hand, the deliberate interrogation of every member of the staff would be bound to reveal at least the person who had written the article. There was no point, I felt, in submitting my colleagues, who had nothing to do with my actions, to this type of pressure if we could help it. In any case, we had no means of knowing what information could have been dredged up; indeed, we did not really know at the time what was on the mind of the authorities. Certainly this was one in a long line of intimidatory acts which might be just another bluff.

We agreed that the staff should be instructed to say as little as possible; that if they were questioned by the police they were to return the exact truth, but not to volunteer any information. I did not think that any person besides myself and the editor knew the identity of my source, but we could never be sure. The one thing that was certain was that had the information got out, it would have caused a far greater furore — on an international scale — than anything we liked to imagine. To this day, as far as I am aware, only three people as well as myself know the full facts: my source, Rhys Meier and my wife.

I said I was prepared to let my name be given to the police as the writer of the story. Rhys Meier looked me in the eye. He had a dark and gimlet glare that pinned you back in your seat; and a voice like a nutmeg grater. It took a long time to know him well enough to learn that he really had a soft centre.

"You realise what the consequences may be?" he said. "It will be entirely up to you whether you give the information or not."

I said that my decision was, and always would be, that the source should not be revealed. John Hennessy promised the company's full support should any legal action ensue. I left the conference with a light step and the scent of battle in my nostrils. It looked like being a good scrap. It turned into an eleven-month war of attrition. Boredom, more than anything else, was to bring me nearest to surrender.

The next day I was interrogated for an hour or so at Salisbury's main police station, in the presence of the company's solicitor. I liked Chief Superintendent May a great deal; he obviously disliked the job he had been given to do and did it with extreme politeness. He and his colleague questioned me closely on every aspect of my story. I told them everything I could, with the exception of any details that could possibly lead to my source. They confiscated all my notes and the story I had written, on *Sunday Mail* copy paper edged with green ink. Supt. May informed me that he believed me to be liable to prosecution under the Official Secrets Act of Rhodesia on two counts; each of them carrying a maximum penalty of four years imprisonment.

Would I please answer his questions? Sorry, no.

Well, then, he would take further advice on the matter, and I would be hearing from him again.

My memory is a little hazy on this point, but I believe that I was questioned in all three times by the police. There was no question of coercion, no question of undue pressure; no question even of impoliteness on their part. After all, they were fishing in waters as unknown to them as they were to me. We just went round in circles, returning always to the point where my "No" began to sound like Mr. Molotov's "Niet", returning repeatedly to those prospective charges. But nothing happened for six weeks. Except that my telephone bill trebled.

We couldn't understand why the usual monthly bill for a fiver or so should suddenly read £15. It was not explained by my activities as a freelance journalist, as these had always been included before and in any case most of my long-distance calls were made "collect". None of my sons had acquired a girl friend in Timbuctoo or even in Bulawayo; and there was no reason to suspect that our servants had suddenly been bitten by the 'phone bug.

We noticed that for some reason it was taking longer to receive the dialling tone when we picked up the receiver. We heard strange noises of clicks and buzzes; heavy breathing interfered with our calls. I checked with a telecommunications expert who worked for Philips in Rhodesia, and he confirmed my suspicions. If the telephone was in proper working order, there was no conceivable reason why the bill should be trebled, unless someone was tampering with the line.

The penny dropped. We were being "bugged". Our efficient Rhodesian police had slipped in a "tap" on our line, but had placed it in front of the meter at the sub-station, not behind it. Every time they switched in to listen to our conversations, another "tichey" (3d) clicked over the meter.

The tapping of private conversations and "bugging" were not really new to Rhodesia. Welensky had used electronic methods to "bug" Dr Hastings Banda when he was in jail in Gwelo back in 1959. But the vastly increased use of this method of obtaining information was new. Our own experiences were unspectacular compared with those of, for example, the Rev David Jenkins, a militant Anglican Churchman, who made one call close on the heels of another, only to hear his first conversation being played back to him over the line . . . Or with those of Brian Raath, a liberal-minded television producer who learnt from a friend in the Salisbury CID that his every movement for the past two weeks had been plotted and recorded at headquarters, including his unscheduled visits to various girl friends . . . But we felt we were unique in being asked to cough up for our own telephone to be tapped.

I refused to pay. I sent the telephone department a cheque for the average monthly amount accompanied by a rude letter. The Post Office were apologetic, but adamant. They sent a charming young electrician to check over the telephone. He came and went for around a fortnight, presumably making the necessary adjustments before he left. All through he stoutly denied to Margaret, who gave him cups of tea every day, that there was any sort of "bug" around.

"We don't do that sort of thing," he protested repeatedly. When he left for the last time he repeated his assurance. "We don't do any bugging," he said, "but I should be careful what you say over the phone . . ."

Margaret, who had occupied most of her telephone time for the past few weeks in baiting our unseen listeners, let it go. She would pick up the receiver, listen to the clicks and buzzes and say. "For God's sake give me a line . . ." It was unfailing. Click, and on came the dialling tone. Then she would hold the most intimate of gynaecological conversations with one of her woman friends and before hanging up ask the unknown listener, sweetly: "Did that help you?"

In June, however, we had a surprise. The Post Office sent me a letter. It was one of those cyclostyled things that government departments use to brush off complaints. There were spaces for the relevant details to be inserted. It read:

Dear sir/Madam;

Your complaint of.........................(date) has been received. The telephone instrument and fitting have been thoroughly checked and have been found to be in order.

It is not possible, therefore, to reduce the account and the outstanding amount of...................must be settled by.........................(date).

Yours faithfully,

.............................(for PMG)

Or words to that effect.

In our case the second paragraph had been deleted. A note in a girlish clerkly hand was scrawled alongside it: "550 test calls have been credited to your June account."

We felt honours were even. But we guarded our tongues on the phone after that.

I was followed, too, wherever I went, and when I ventured into the National Club, or the Long Bar at Meikles, or the Ambassador or wherever, there was usually a Special Branch man on hand. Salisbury is a small city and one gets to know many people. If I did not recognise my "tail" personally, one of my colleagues would warn me. I usually paid little attention, but if the efforts became too crude we felt it proper occasionally to bite back. Ken Brokensha and I once led a gentleman with particularly large feet for two hours through four major stores in the centre of the town, and finally waved him good-bye from the steps of the *Sunday Mail* office. The temperature was in the high seventies, and he was limping. Even more blatant attempts were made by our friends in the Rhodesian Information Department to monitor my off-duty conversations. Much good may it have done them; they bought the drinks.

It is easy now to be flippant, but it was for all of us a time of gathering tension. In conversation with our lawyers I discovered a number of interesting but scarcely comforting facts about the Rhodesian Secrets Act. It was very similar in its scope and in its vagueness to the British Official Secrets Act of 1911, on which it was based. That particular Act had been devised after a civil servant had divulged a certain piece of paper *to a journalist.* It was always my contention that we were not dealing with a secret document that could be of use to an enemy of the Rhodesian state; but with an economic document based on a hypothetical situation that was of vital interest to Rhodesian citizens. But Professor Dick Christie QC, whom we engaged to defend me should the worst come to the worst, informed me that under the law *any* document could be declared secret by the Government should it so wish, including yesterday's newspaper.

However, what worried Christie and the lawyers, and henceforth me, was not so much a direct prosecution under the Official Secrets Act. We felt that we had such a strong moral case on this front that the government would be most unwise to attempt to press home a technical conviction – even if they could get one. But there was another and much more subtle way by which the government might want to increase the pressure both on me and on my employers. Rhodesian law is a mixture of the British and the Romano-Dutch codes, and tucked away in the legacy from the old Cape Province is a provision, Section 131 of the Public Order Act.

Section 131 substitutes for what is more popularly known in Britain as "contempt of court". Under it, the public prosecutor in Rhodesia, *if he believes a crime to have been committed,* can summons a person he believes to be a witness to that crime before a magistrate, and question him in court. (Note that the public prosecutor – i.e. the police – does not have to *prove* that a crime has been committed.)

If the unfortunate witness declines to answer, under Section 131 the Magistrate has the power to commit him to prison for up to seven days. At the end of that time, the witness can be taken back to the court and questioned again; and the whole process repeated "until the witness does as the court requires".

This is much wider than the British provisions for punishment of contempt of court. Seven days jail sounds little enough, but seven days recurring "until the witness does as the court requires" is in effect an indefinite sentence without the necessity of a charge being laid. In Britain you can "purge your contempt" by your spell in jail, be it ever so long.

Six weeks after Superintendent May had first stumped into our office, I received a large green foolscap summons. It required me to attend a Salisbury court to answer certain questions in connection with a suspected offence under the Official Secrets Act.

I came quite to like Superintendent May and the other Rhodesian policemen with whom I was dealing. They certainly had a distaste for what they were trying to make me do, and made it very clear that this was a matter being pressed by the politicians rather than the police. It was an attitude shared by many of the departments with whom I came in contact over the next few months. The vigour and persistence with which the case was pursued convinced me that it was all part of the campaign against the Press. The Government thought they had us over a barrel. By this time the case was becoming something of a *cause célèbre*. If we talked, then the country would know that it could not trust the word of a journalist. If we did not do so, then the Government was able to demonstrate how the traitorous Press was defying the law. The fact that they had by chance ensnared the President of the Guild of Journalists was a bonus for Smith and his colleagues. I do not think that the government held any personal animus at that time towards me, although my former colleague Harvey Ward had been heard at several cocktail parties to mutter menacingly: "We'll have Parker thrown out . . ."

At first, it seemed as if the government was going to have all its own way. I was duly arraigned before a Mr

Barnes, a Salisbury magistrate who found the whole thing far too hot a potato to handle and who treated me and everyone else in the case with the softest of kid gloves. At the time I thought the Public Prosecutor a bit of a bastard, but I suppose he was only doing his duty. My real irritation was reserved for Dick Christie, my Counsel, who seemed to be trying his best to ensure that I spent the next few years behind bars. Of course he was doing nothing of the sort, but I felt that he was at least three parts convinced that I would be forced to reveal my source in the end, so what was the use of fighting the battle anyway? He rode roughshod over my wishes as to the way the case was to be handled and persisted in regaling the court with a history of the Official Secrets Act and the journalists who had gone to jail for transgressing it. With every sentence I could see the doors of the prison looming larger. Christie made no attempt to challenge the prosecutor's assumption that a crime had been committed and little attempt to establish any form of justification for my stand or the stand of my company. Since the company was paying him to defend me on their behalf his efforts seemed to me to be distinctly lacking in both skill and enthusiasm.

However, he did manage to lodge an appeal after Mr Barnes, almost apologetically, had told me that I would have to go to prison for 48 hours. The Magistrate declined to use the full seven days' term as allowed in the law in the hope that two days would be sufficient to ensure that this attitude of mine did not persist. He even went so far as to say he both understood and more or less agreed with my stand, which could not have done his promotion prospects much good. In any case, he agreed with alacrity that I could appeal, and that I should not go to jail pending the result of that appeal. The Prosecutor was so abashed that he forgot to ask me to surrender my travel documents, passport and so on. However, I had no intention of ducking out of the fight.

The appeal was heard in July in the small, panelled Rhodesian High Court. Three venerable be-wigged gentlemen were sitting behind a high desk at one end of the cramped room. Messrs Stumbles, Lewis and Macdonald, listening to Counsel's argument for a day and a half, questioning and cross-questioning; but it was obvious from the opening words which way it was going to go. An adjournment "sine die", and then a recall some three weeks later to hear the verdict: appeal dismissed. A nasty rider from Mr Justice Macdonald to the effect that a journalist is a citizen and must accept a citizen's responsibilities and expect no special protection from the courts. I was to be committed immediately to prison for 48 hours; thence to be taken back to the Magistrate's Court and asked the questions again. Unless, that is, I cared to answer the Court now. No, My Lord, with respect, my client declines to answer the questions.

A polite policeman reluctantly allowed me back to my office to tidy up my desk, and I was escorted to the main Salisbury Police Station and thence to Salisbury Prison.

There, they didn't really know what to do with me. They hadn't had a prisoner like me before, so they locked me away in solitary confinement for my 48 hours. I was allowed no contact with the other inmates — I don't know who was supposed to be corrupting whom — but a succession of disembodied voices through the peephole in the door alternately cadged my cigarettes and boosted my morale.

"Psst!"

A knowing eye at the peephole.

"What you in for?"

"Refusing to talk to the police"

"Don't tell them bastards anything; Got a snout?"

The prison was racially segregated, like other social amenities. In the morning I was taken down at about 6.30 to a small exercise yard with 20 foot high unscaleable walls. For half an hour I was allowed to breathe in the fresh air and pace about, listening to the sounds of the morning beatings going on over the wall. This appeared to be corporal punishment time, when the unfortunate victims received their cuts with the birch, and the weeping struck hard across the sunlit mornings. I shall also remember the food, which I received in solitary and half an hour after everyone else. By this time it had congealed into a cold mass of sadza (mealie meal) porridge and gravy; and I confined myself to eating the biscuits and chocolate that I had brought in with me. Some brave souls declared they would send in oranges injected with gin, in order to keep my spirits up as it were, but if they did the oranges never reached me. Perhaps it was as well, for I had plenty of time to think. I thought about the case.

By this time Dick Christie had given me up as a bad job and had withdrawn; in his place we had found Michael May, a quietly-spoken QC with a fine record. He was undoubtedly one of the foremost Counsel in Southern Africa, and I owe a great deal to his patient advocacy. He had cause to be patient at times, indeed, for I was not the easiest of clients. But he agreed with my thinking that the real weakness in the Crown case against me was that there was no genuine proof that the Public Prosecutor had grounds to believe that a crime had been committed, under the Official Secrets or any other Act. He had very little time to prepare a case, indeed, for I was only inside jail for the statutory 48 hours before I was escorted back into court.

This time it was not the friendly Mr Barnes, but a Magistrate of a very different way of thinking. He wasted no time in hauling me into the box, snapping the questions at me, and re-committing me to jail for seven days. But this time too I did not have the bumbling Dick Christie, but Michael May on my side. He insisted on calling fresh evidence, and a most bad-tempered magistrate eventually allowed him to do so.

For the first time, May produced evidence from officials of the Chamber of Commerce and the Association of Industries on how these reports had been prepared; and who had access to them. He pointed out that there were literally scores of persons who had seen the documents; at least 30 of them non-civil servants. This was an important point because the public prosecutor's questioning of me had made it plain that he believed the original leak to have come from the Civil Service — a point which I had denied. The evidence made no difference to the Magistrate. Back to jail I was to go; and it took Michael May an hour to persuade him to allow me the right of appeal. It took at least another 40 minutes for May to persuade him to agree to my being released pending the hearing of the second appeal, but he did so eventually with the utmost bad grace after May had pointed out that the legal process might mean that I could spend an indefinite time in jail — on no charge — awaiting the result of an appeal that could well release me. Had he failed at this stage, May was preparing to bring in a writ of *habeas corpus,* but it turned out not to be necessary.

So the date was set for the second appeal; November 16. As it turned out, it was the day after Smith made his declaration of independence; and it was a point of serious discussion whether the Appeal Court would sit at all. But sit it did and at the appointed hour the three judges trooped in and the battle started all over again. May's argument was quietly effective, I thought; but the Crown Counsel, to my astonishment, rested his entire case on the result of the first appeal. He disregarded totally May's new arguments and evidence, hardly bothering to mention them, and launched a bitter attack on journalists and the press on the lines of Macdonald's rider in the first judgement.

Two days before Christmas we gathered again to hear the result of the appeal. Before it, May called me in and told me that it was his considered legal opinion that we had about 20 per cent chance of success; and that if we did fail, it was his duty to advise me that, legally, I should talk and disclose my sources. I am afraid I shouted at him; as I did at both Rhys Meier and Jack Slater when they gave me the same advice. But the necessity never arose.

To my complete astonishment, and to that of Michael May, the Court totally reversed their earlier opinion. Not only was the appeal upheld against my committal to jail, but it was stated in another unanimous rider to the judgment that I had been "subjected to unwarranted persecution by police and courts."

Three weeks later, a friendly government official knocked on my door late one night.

"I have to tell you that you are going to be deported." he said. "This is unofficial — you won't get the papers until next week. See if you can do anything."

The Parkers' stay in Rhodesia had nearly ended.

Governments rarely give reasons for declaring any particular individual *persona non grata* and no exception was made in my case. I do not flatter myself that I could have been considered an enemy of the state, even the illegally declared Republic of Rhodesia. One can only assume that I had become an embarrassment to the regime, particularly after winning the case against it. It was quicker, cleaner and easier to eliminate the opposition I represented, however small, than to bother to fight it any more.

On the other hand, my case had evoked a great deal of sympathy both in Rhodesia and abroad, and the Rhodesian Front was concerned to eliminate anyone who might act as a rallying point for moderate liberal opinion. I received constant messages of support from both individuals and organisations overseas. The British National Union of Journalists cabled me offering assistance should it be necessary, and *The Times* of London, for whom I had corresponded for four years in Salisbury, sent their Commonwealth Correspondent with a touching message. Roy Lewis was a staunch friend all through the various tensions and he told me, albeit with his usual tongue in cheek: "I'm instructed to let you know that should the Rhodesian Government persist with this monstrous prosecution, the full weight of *The Times* will be behind you."

The Rhodesian Government could afford to take a calculated risk on overseas opinion, but it still did not want to create any more martyrs than it had already. I was better off out of the country, so far as they were concerned.

I rather agree with them.

CHAPTER EIGHT

A Matter of Principles?

One of the most remarkable features about that crowded year that led up to UDI was that life managed to go on in addition to everything else. There were school examinations to be passed, swimming galas to attend, a couple of doses of glandular fever in the family; and my fourth son Paul fell off the roof and broke both wrists. He was lucky to be alive. Margaret, who had become a personality presenting advertisements on Rhodesian Television, gave up her job to have our sixth and last baby; after five boys our daughter was born and all was right in our personal little world.

But what was happening in society around us kept encroaching, building up in my mind straw by straw a tentative conviction that soon now I would have to leave Rhodesia. In retrospect my somewhat fatalistic attitude towards the court case could well have been inspired by the thought that I had not long to go as a Rhodesian. There were two major reasons for this.

On my own account I could foresee that I would not be able to stand still politically. By accepting the challenge to my own idea of the journalistic ethic I had publicly declared myself to be opposed to the Rhodesian Front, which meant to the majority of the people among whom I lived and worked. In their terms, this branded me "traitor" anyway. The number of invitations to official receptions fell away sharply, as was to be expected. What I didn't anticipate was the fact that my demonstration of resistance to governmental pressure should gain me acceptance, in the eyes of both liberal whites and nationalist blacks, as "one of them". One example will, I think illustrate the point.

Some time after the case first became public, I took Roy Lewis of *The Times* and Lionel Fleming, representing the *Irish Times*, to the Wha Wha restriction camp near Gwelo to see the Reverend Ndabaninge Sithole and his fellow ZANU restrictees. It was a long, hot, day.

Wha Wha was something like 70 or 80 miles from Gwelo, and we reached it after a six hour drive by Land Rover from Salisbury. We picked up an African sergeant of police in Gwelo, as we had been instructed to do by the authorities. He was to keep an eye on us and to report back our conversation. By the time we arrived the Land Rover, and our persons, were covered from head to toe with a half-inch layer of choking red dust. We were greeted cheerfully enough, if suspiciously, until I told them my name. On the instant, suspicion fell away, Leopold Takawira appeared with a wide-mouthed grinning Enos Nkala, and we were ushered (a precise description) into the presence of Sithole.

The camp was a clutch of small corrugated iron shanties scattered around in the dry brown Rhodesian bush, their silver newness contrasting strongly with the cracked bare earth and twisted grey mopani trees. There was dust everywhere under a burnished sky. We were led through the defensive hedge the detainees had cut themselves for protection from marauding elephant and buffalo, great bunches of impenetrable thorn piled on each other eight feet high and more.

Sithole stood waiting outside his double-sized hut in its own clearing, the ground swept bare around with military efficiency. Sithole was larger than I remembered him, different altogether from the amiably sharp-witted clergyman I had known slightly at liberal sundowner parties in Alexandra Park and the Jameson Hotel. Bigger, blacker, more beetle-browed and much more formidable.

"Wait," he said. "I will not speak to you until you appear as white men."

We were led around to the back of the hut. There, on a crude wooden bench, were three brand-new aluminium bowls, each filled to the brim with clear cold water. Alongside each was folded a new white towel and a fresh bar of soap.

After washing we were given a complete account of the plans of the Zimbabwe African National Union while our sergeant, who knew his place in such society, was relieved to be sent off to help drink some of the beer we had brought with us.

That these plans have hardly matured, that ZANU under-estimated the Rhodesian security's intelligence system, that their hopes have not been fulfilled, do not matter in this context. What does was that they were prepared to reveal to two complete strangers and one who was at best a nodding acquaintance some of their most detailed secrets on the strength of the knowledge that one of their visitors was prepared to stand up against the regime. They were prepared to identify me on a precisely similar basis to that on which I was recognised by the Rhodesian Front. The white supremacist said: "If you're not with us you're against us." The African nationalist interpreted it: "If you're against them you must be with us."

Taking the argument a stage further, I could see myself being drawn further and further into a position which I would find intolerable. I was fast coming to believe that the only way the African in Rhodesia would ever attain his goal of political freedom and equality with the white man was through the use of force. Nothing that has happened in the past six years since UDI has led me to change my mind, I feel it more strongly than ever. But I felt equally strongly that I did not wish to be part of such violence, although I could see quite plainly the course which both whites and blacks had laid out in front of me.

I was by now convinced that the African demand for

political freedom was just. Sympathy was leading to friendship, and friendship would inevitably lead to assistance. Put bluntly, this was involvement, and once involved in the nationalist cause there could be no turning back. It would be "boots and all" into the violence which must inevitably grow one day to a bloody climax. Put even more bluntly, it was no great step to visualise myself planning – and even executing – political murder.

I am a coward. Violence is anathema to me. The prospect of inflicting physical suffering on another human being is only slightly less repulsive than the prospect of someone else inflicting pain on me. I will cross the road to avoid a strange dog, and the thought of entering a field of cows makes my palms sweat. I am no hero, nor am I a saint. I yield to no-one in my admiration for the massive moral strength of a man like Guy Clutton-Brock, who held out the hand of friendship to the African at Cold Comfort Farm for so many years in defiance of the authorities without ever a hint of violence. But his way is not for me. I just can't take it.

Because I dislike violence and intrigue, I certainly wouldn't be very good at it. Which would be sure to lead sooner rather than later to being caught – another consideration. It's one thing to march Lawrence-like into the capital of the oppressor at the head of your cheering thousands; it's quite another to endure the sweat, the fear and the years of danger and despair which must go into the winning of the struggle.

Another easy alibi for me was the family, a good enough reason for running away from a personal situation which looked like getting out of hand. But there was more to it than that. My six children, three of them born Rhodesian, had had the good fortune to spend their early days in something like idyllic conditions. They were healthy, intelligent and good-looking. What was to be *their* future?

Already we had had some evidence of the pressure of society upon the boys which would in the end force them to make exactly the same choice as was facing me and the rest of white Rhodesians. Fortunately there were too many of them and they were too large and athletic for schoolboy-type bullying to have much effect. Guy (aged 11) came home one day in some perturbation with a drawing of a man hanging from a scaffold. It had been presented to him by a friend who told him: "That's what my father says your father should be doing." Guy, who weighed 10lb when born and has maintained the differential since, deposited him in a ditch with a bloody nose and I forebore to lecture him on the evils of violence.

Neil and Nigel, at senior school, had one or two scraps but this only hardened them in their support of my stand. They came back with glee one day to tell us that the masters, in an endeavour to release some of the political tension which was generating throughout the school, had organised water-polo matches throughout the age-groups on a pro- and anti-Front basis. The results didn't matter, but the interesting point was the division of the teams. By far the majority of the pro-Fronters were from the C and D streams; the A and B streams made up the bulk of the "antis".

But I knew my sons would inevitably be forced to make the choice between the two extremes, white or black, suppression or revolution. In the climate which I could foresee there was only one thing to do, to remove them from the country and let them at a later stage make up their own minds about whether they would go back or not. I wanted my sons to be neither left-wing revolutionaries nor right-wing supremacists as a result of *my* actions. I wanted them to be able to make up their own minds.

It was also highly probable, I felt, that the growing isolationist tendencies of the Rhodesian leaders would over a long period inhibit the training and development of youngsters, regardless of their colour. In fact it seems that this has happened. There are multiplying reports that Rhodesian teenagers are finding the opportunities within the country so limited (in comparison with the free-for-all chances of the boom days) that they no longer see their future within the country and are leaving in their hundreds.

More significant still is that the natural increase of the white Rhodesian population has dropped in the six years since UDI to well under two per cent. This can only mean that the average European is getting older — he's now well over 40. The white Rhodesian has lost his confidence in the future he intends to pass on to his children and grandchildren.

At the same time, the African rate of increase is rising; it is now 3.6 per cent. *More Africans are born in Rhodesia every year than the entire white population.*

It is a sentence that should be engraved upon the heart of every white man in the country. At the current rate of progress, by the end of the century, assuming the highest levels of immigration possible for Rhodesia to absorb, there will be more than 20 million Africans in Rhodesia and under one million Europeans.

I cannot pretend that these were positive lines of thinking at the time I received that knock on the door on January 1966, and the Rhodesian government made up my mind for me. Sir Roy Welensky has told me several times since: "They did the best turn anyone's done for you in your life. There's no future in my country now."

He may well be right, but that does not stop us from dwelling on what might have been.

A unilateral declaration by Ian Smith and the Rhodesian Front government of Rhodesia was inevitable from the day in 1964 when Sir Alec Douglas-Home, then Conservative Prime Minister, laid down the famous "five principles" upon which Britain was prepared to *grant* independence. They were subsequently endorsed and strengthened by Labour's Harold Wilson, who became the target for every smear the limited Rhodesian invention could place upon him.

Once these principles were stated, the whole ritual dance, with successive visits from British Ministers to Salisbury, culminating in Wilson's odyssey, was unnecessary. So too were the two trips Smith made to London and so too were the extraordinary meetings between Smith and Wilson first on the *Tiger* and then on the *Fearless*. For the "five principles" conflict directly with what Ian Smith and the Rhodesian Front believe in.

In the earlier days, when some form of a progressive attitude was *de rigeur*, the Front played their role cautiously. Ian Smith's approach to UDI itself was a great game of brinkmanship in which he appeared to be teetering on the edge of a decision and then pulling back from it. Eventually the white electorate were so punch-drunk from the continuing contrived political crises that they would have voted for the devil himself if he offered to put an end to uncertainty. But Smith used the time to purge the civil service and set the climate for the extremists to take over. Once the African nationalists were removed from the public gaze and the Press sufficiently cowed, the bullies were given full rein.

Those of us who hoped that sanity would prevail over white supremacy clung to the hope that Britain would be able to check the madness, long after it was apparent that the former Colonial power had nothing left in the kitty in the way of strength and little indeed of resolution. Those Africans who begged, prayed and demanded that Britain should use force to quell the white rebellion totally overestimated Britain's ability to intervene.

It is probably true that a couple of parachute battalions dropped on Salisbury airport the day after UDI would have been adequate force to end the rebellion; despite the purges at the top there was still the utmost doubt that the white Rhodesian forces would have fought back, and Rhodesia's black battalions had been disarmed in case they should turn on their masters. There would have been some fairly tough guerrilla fighting with the odd farmers — indeed these gentlemen had with some relish cast themselves in the role of the Boers who made things so uncomfortable for the British back in the days of Queen Victoria and prepared their farmsteads as if for siege.

Two statements were made at the time of UDI which their authors must have regretted daily ever since. The first was Harold Wilson's assurance to the assembled Prime

Ministers of the Commonwealth in Lagos in January 1966 that sanctions would bring the Rhodesian rebel regime to its knees "in a matter of weeks, not months." The second was Ian Smith's assurance to his supporters that UDI would be a matter of a "three-days wonder in the City of London." Patently, neither prophecy was fulfilled.

It is not fashionable in 1972 to ascribe to Mr Wilson the qualities of steadfastness and consistency. But in spite of all his detractors say, in the Rhodesian issue he has possessed both.

When he was voted into power in 1964, Harold Wilson knew little enough about African affairs. His visit to Rhodesia at the end of October 1965 was as much a fact-finding mission for him as it was an attempt to stall Smith from declaring his UDI. But what Wilson found in Salisbury during that visit set him upon the course that he has followed ever since, wavering only momentarily during the *Tiger* and the *Fearless* talks.

His statement made at the end of his Salisbury visit remains the definitive case against the white Rhodesian. It should be compulsory reading for anyone who wishes to understand the basic moral reason why the British government embarked on sanctions when it found itself unable to use force; and why the world has maintained them for six years in the face of apparent and comparative failure.

The apologists for the Smith regime, like its propagandists, call for the end of sanctions on a number of grounds. They say sanctions have failed to bring down the regime, have failed to affect the standard of living of the white man and have merely depressed the standards of those they are designed to help, the Africans. However, if sanctions have been such a failure, then why should there be such continuing pressure to have them lifted?

Rhodesia is a producing country. It can feed itself adequately and have plenty left over. Even in a drought year like 1970 it did not go hungry. The regime has physical control over the country by force of arms and is backed by South African power; in South Africa and

Portugal its sea-ward neighbours it has two like-minded regimes who have broken and will continue to break the sanctions barrier.

But it is also true that sanctions have bitten deep into the Rhodesian economy and have held the regime back from profiting fully after UDI. Even in 1971, six years after, the economy had not yet recovered to the level it enjoyed in 1965, the year before UDI. In a developing country in which the growth rate had averaged approaching ten per cent for the previous 15 years, this means that it, ie the economy is currently fifty per cent behind its probable position had UDI not been declared.

The tobacco industry has been virtually destroyed. Even on Rhodesian figures, £40,000,000 worth of tobacco lies rotting in great hangars on Belvedere airport near Salisbury; the true figure is probably twice as much. Two-thirds of the country's white farmers are bankrupt and living on subsidies provided by the Government. Exports of copper and chrome and other minerals keep the Rhodesian economy afloat but not forging ahead. The shortage of foreign currency is severely limiting imports of both luxury and essential goods, forcing the economy to diversify although at the same time severely inhibiting development. All this is the "belt-tightening" which Ian Smith forecast would be a "three-day wonder."

At the same time, in spite of sanctions, the white man in Rhodesia has been able largely to maintain his "way of life", even though he has to make his car last two or three years instead of getting a new one very year; although his Rose's Lime Marmalade has given way to Cashel Valley Products and his Scotch may have strange labels. Restrictions on foreign exchange and the lack of significant development projects mean that there is a large surplus of liquid money. This in turn has led to the biggest building boom Rhodesia has seen since the early 'fifties; houses have mushroomed throughout the city suburbs, mortgages have become available at giveaway rates and you can buy a swimming pool over twenty years or even longer, without a deposit. The "Rhodesian Way of Life" is maintained no matter what the cost.

Derek Ingram, head of the Gemini News Service in London, who visited Rhodesia three years after UDI, wrote: "Salisbury looks just the same as it did three years ago. It just seems twenty years older." Under the surface success he detected a cynicism which had replaced the heady idealism of the days of UDI. Six years of sanctions have destroyed the white Rhodesian's ability to hold up his head in the world. Once-proud businessmen have become accustomed to dealing with the sleazy international underworld of middle-men, customs-evaders and currency fixers. Rhodesian goods, formerly proudly marketed across five continents, sneak into strange places in plain wrappers, leaving behind a string of forged documents. Rhodesian travellers "wangle" South African passports in order to pass from one country to another: possession of the Rhodesian passport, once an object of envy because it was just that bit "different" is now a distinct drawback in nine countries out of ten.

Rhodesia claims to be the most peaceful nation in Africa; and yet it still maintains the state of emergency which was instituted four days before UDI. It claims to be educating more Africans than any other country in the continent apart from South Africa; and yet over ninety per cent of the children who go to school never get past the primary stage. It claims to be the last bastion of "British traditions" in Africa; and yet its African political leaders have been in detention for more than six years.

Possibly by the time this book is published, the British government will have concluded its shameful exercise of disengagement from the Rhodesian problem. The Conservative Foreign Minister, Sir Alec Douglas-Home, was the man who first defined the famous Five Principles and he has now signed his name to a set of proposals which, even if they are carried out with scrupulous honesty by the Rhodesian regime, totally fail to meet the requirements of any single one of those principles.

It is worth re-stating them.

1. The principle and intention of unimpeded progress to

majority rule, already enshrined in the 1961 Constitution, would have to be maintained and guaranteed.

2. There would have to be guarantees against retrogressive amendment of the Constitution.
3. There would have to be immediate improvement in the political status of the African.
4. There would have to be progress towards ending racial discrimination.
5. The British Government would need to be satisfied that any basis proposed for independence was acceptable to the people of Rhodesia as a whole.

(Harold Wilson added a sixth, which the Tories conveniently forgot. It was: That there should be no intimidation of the minority by the majority, or of the majority by the minority. Perhaps Sir Alec thought it unimportant.) Taking them one at a time, and very briefly:

Principle One. The *principle* of majority rule has been consistently denied by the white Rhodesians (with the exception of a few who are called left-wing extremists) before and since UDI; before, during and after the negotiations on *Tiger*, *Fearless* and in Salisbury. The statements by Smith, and other white Rhodesians, since the settlement proposals were agreed can leave no-one in the slightest doubt that they have no *intention* of conceding majority rule now or at any other time. The whole deal, in place of providing *unimpeded* progress towards majority rule, is packed with *impediments* to ensure that no person now alive will see majority rule in Rhodesia.

Principle Two. The sole guarantee against retrogressive amendment of the Constitution (which, heaven knows, hardly requires it anyway to stop the blacks from ever attaining their object) is the good faith of Smith, his government, his party and his successors. One must be forgiven for doubting the efficacy of such a "guarantee."

Principle Three: There is no immediate improvement offered in political status for the African. Some thousands more may be afforded the opportunity to register on the lower African roll by a reduction in qualifications, but *they will not elect one more MP.* The creation of a higher African roll with equal qualifications to those of the European immediately worsens the political status of the African people, whose wages, education and social status are already deliberately depressed by Rhodesian apartheid. **Principle Four** There is no progress towards the ending of racial discrimination. The Rhodesian regime has undertaken to accept a Commission to "investigate" discrimination and to "recommend" its findings to Parliament. But not one thing has been done to reverse the trend to apartheid which has become increasingly apparent in Rhodesia over the past 20 years, not one racially prejudicial measure is to be altered. In fact, by enshrining separate African and European rolls in the Constitution the proposals establish discrimination at the very heart of the political system.

Principle Five: If the Pearce Commission which is investigating "acceptability" comes to the conclusion that the proposals are acceptable to the majority of the "people of Rhodesia as a whole", then they will have failed totally to do their job with either insight or honesty. Having watched with growing dismay the spectacle of Sir Alec Douglas-Home and Lord Goodman committing political hypocrisy on a scale amounting to depravity I suppose one must be conditioned to expect anything.

There is little consolation left now for those of us who hoped and dreamed for a place in the sun for all who live and have their being in the land Rhodes wrenched from Lobengula. It is small compensation to know at last that Britain will be out of it; that the destiny of Rhodesia now rests upon the little white island of 250,000 whites in the sea of five million blacks. Britain reneged on her power years ago; now she has reneged on her responsibility and to the eternal discredit of Mr Heath and Sir Alec Douglas-Home has presented the settlement proposals as a "triumph".

It is not so much a sell-out as a give-away of the rights and future of five million human beings. As *The Sunday Times* put it, an ignoble way to end an empire. But if the final hurdle towards an agreement is brushed aside and the white Rhodesians achieve the badge of respectablity and the end of the burden of sanctions, I wonder if the champagne and the rejoicing will be deemed worth it in the blood-bath that will follow as inexorably as night follows day.

The foundation of the police state is force; and Smith and his followers base their strength on the rock of security. Military dominance of her black neighbours to the north, the grip of the police and the army on the population at home are the twin bases of the European confidence in the future. With the ending of the last shreds of British influence, there are ominous signs of a strengthening of African resolve and an ending to the almost totally disabling internecine struggles between the African nationalist parties themselves. The efforts of the African nationalists have often been treated with contempt both by the whites of Rhodesia and South Africa and by the nations of the Organisation of African Unity. But the remarkable thing is not that the African spirit has raised its voice so rarely, but that it has been able to do so at all and that it continues to do so. In 1968 the most serious incursions so far into the Zambesi Valley kept the Rhodesian forces at full stretch for some months; the Rhodesians themselves reluctantly acknowledged that 13 members of the security forces had been killed; in return they claimed hundreds of guerrilla "terrorists" wiped out. But the direct result of that year was that South Africa was for the first time allowed into Rhodesia to help maintain the line against black nationalism. South African security patrols have been working alongside Rhodesians ever since, on the pretext that they have a direct interest in the link-up between members of the Rhodesian ZAPU and the South African ANC, who combined forces to mount the most effective thrusts into Rhodesian territory. Periodic guerrilla trials and the equally spasmodic discoveries of arms caches which somehow leak into the Press give the impression at least that white Rhodesians scarcely sleep more easily in their beds for six years of their make-believe "independence".

It is perhaps too early for Ian Smith and his 200,000 white followers, many of whom were my friends and neighbours, to admit to themselves the truth of what they have done. In the name of preserving freedom they have destroyed it. In choosing their own destiny they have handed their fate over to the people they profess to despise.

For the future of Rhodesia no longer lies in the hands of the Europeans. It is not a question now of if, but when and how, the Africans will take over. *More Africans are born every year than there are Europeans in the country. More Africans leave school each year than there are European workers in employment.* Rhodesia is a pressure cooker with the lid screwed down by the Europeans, and it will blow up in their faces.

When we first arrived in Bulawayo in 1955, there was the possibility for Europeans and Africans to work together for the future of this potentially rich and lovely country. Rhodesia was indeed the "land of opportunity". But the years have passed and the opportunity has gone — so far as we were concerned it passed us by almost before we realised it was there. UDI was the practical end to the dream of "partnership"; all that has happened since has been the locking of the door and the barring of the windows against any form of racial progress.

Now all that is left for the Europeans of Rhodesia is to cling on to their "way of life" while they can; to judge the future more clearly than they have the past and to run while there is anywhere to run to. South Africa will still be there, a haven for a year or two after Rhodesia, and maybe Australia will have them after that.

Unless, of course, the African leaders of a future Zimbabwe are to be more magnanimous and far-seeing than their European masters have been in the past. There is precious little reason why they should be.

Index

DATE DUE